**Water your garden and watch your mind bloom**
A collection of poems inspired by nature to remind you
—you *are* enough, you *are* strong and you *are* healing.

# water your garden & watch your mind bloom

A collection of poems inspired by nature to remind you
—you are enough, you are strong and you are healing.

## Lissa Larsen

Cover, illustrations and layout: Lissa Larsen
Instagram: _softlyrooted_

Publisher: BoD · Books on Demand, Strandvejen 100,
2900 Hellerup, Denmark, bod@bod.dk
Print: Libri Plureos GmbH, Friedensallee 273,
22763 Hamborg, Germany.

ISBN: 978-87-7170-027-5

I choose *me*.
I choose to come home to *myself*.

Like the flowers in your garden,
don't forget to water your inner child—
with love, with patience, with the gentle hands of care.
Let them bloom in the sunlight they were once denied.

As a child, I learned to shrink myself,
to silence my voice, to tiptoe through a house of thunder—
all to keep a storm from breaking.
But no matter how small I became,
it was never enough.
Nothing was ever enough.

So I grew up before my time,
traded childhood wonder for wisdom
too heavy for small shoulders.
My friends called me *mature*,
but they never saw the wilted petals beneath my smile,
the way I curled inward, hiding from the wind.
They loved my home; I loathed it.
Because they only saw the polished garden,
never the roots tangled in sorrow,
never the invisible scars that ran deep beneath the soil.

For twenty years, I ran—
let anxiety, depression, and grief steer my life,
like weeds creeping through every crack.
But rock bottom has a way of whispering,
*It's time.*
Time to dig my hands into the earth,
to nurture what was once neglected,
to meet the child within me and tell her—
You are enough.
You always were.
You never had to beg for love.

This collection of poems, born from my own garden,
from the rhythm of nature and the love of life,
is a gift—
to my inner child, to my own children,
to anyone who needs to hear it:

*You are enough.*
*You are strong.*
*You are healing.*

# tool box

**A little note before we begin**

This book wanders through some heavy woods—
touching tenderly on themes like childhood trauma,
depression, anxiety, suicidal thoughts, and self-harm.
If these subjects feel too raw or overwhelming for you right
now, it's okay to set this book back on the shelf.
Your well-being comes first, *always.*

That said, these poems aren't just about the shadows—
they're about the slow, stubborn magic of healing.
They speak in the soft language of wildflowers and weather,
of soil and seasons. They're little seeds of kindness, planted
with hope.

So if you're ready to explore the tangled, beautiful mess of
being human—with muddy hands, tear streaked petals,
and sunlight peeking through the leaves—then step in.
Just remember to bring gentleness. Especially for yourself.

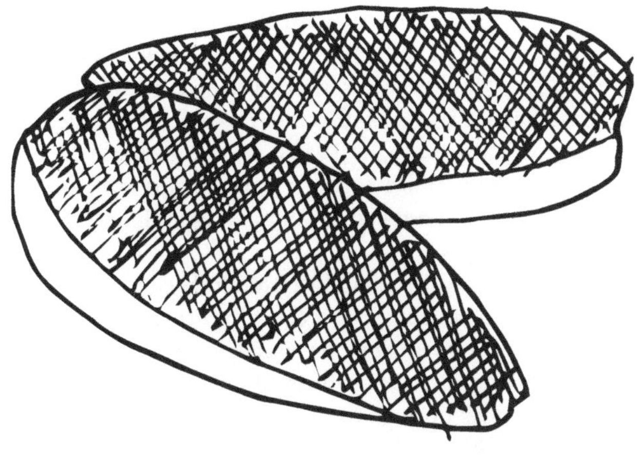

# the seed

There are countless kinds of seeds—some no bigger than a grain of sand, others round and full, some wrapped in delicate casings, and some locked within tough, unyielding shells. Each one carries the promise of life, yet no two awaken in quite the same way. Some seeds, like those of the olive tree, must be sanded down—gently worn, softened by time and touch—before they can drink in the water that will stir them to life. Others, like the whisper-thin lettuce seed, need only the lightest kiss of moisture to awaken.

Isn't it the same with us? We are not made to follow a single, rigid path. Growth is not a "one size fits all" journey. Yes, there are guides, frameworks, and wisdom passed down like ancient soil, but in the end, we must learn through patience, through trial and error, through listening to our own needs. What works for one may not work for another, and that is not failure—it is nature. It is life.

I've seen it in my garden, and I've felt it in my heart. If something no longer serves me, I shift, I try again. The seed does not despair when it takes longer to sprout; it does not compare itself to the seedlings rising beside it. Some seeds break through the soil in mere days, their tiny leaves trembling in the breeze. Others take weeks, even months, resting in the dark before they are ready. But no matter the time it takes, the potential remains. The promise of growth is always there.

So be kind to yourself. No matter how small your progress may seem, no matter how slow your unfolding, you are still growing. You are still reaching. And one day, just like the seed, you will break through, stretching toward the warmth of the sun, stronger than you ever imagined.

"This is such a mess," she mumbles, her voice like a soft
breeze caught in the tangled wildness of her curly hair.
She combs her fingers through the spirals, grounding
herself as her eyes sweep across the table. Seed packets lie
scattered like tiny envelopes of possibility—sunflowers,
chamomile, wild thyme—each one whispering stories of
seasons past and those yet to come.

     She's trying to make sense of it all: the summer
seeds, the winter seeds, the way they once lived separately
in two garden tins, safe and sorted. But now, like a garden
in riotous bloom, they've mingled, entwining roots and
dreams, leaving her with a delightful yet daunting puzzle.
She huffs out a breath, her mind sowing solutions,
and then—a light flickers on inside her. A binder.
That's what she needs. She rummages through her shelves,
fingers grazing over old journals and sketchbooks, until they
land on a green binder, dusty yet sturdy, waiting to be of
service.
She brushes off the thin layer of dust, watching the motes
dance in the sunbeams, tiny faeries swirling in the golden
hour.

Inside the binder are four-sectioned plastic pages,
clear pockets like windows to the future blooms. She smiles,
feeling a sense of rightness as she sets to work, her slender
fingers plucking packets from the chaos and arranging them
by their botanical kinship. She hums a little melody—
something old, something that sounds like spring.

The seeds seem to settle, content with their new order.
An hour passes, and she leans back, letting out a deep,
contented sigh. The binder feels alive now, buzzing with
quiet potential. Her gaze lands on the Posca pens in the
center of the table, and with a spark of inspiration,
she reaches for them, fingers tracing the smooth barrels.
On the binder's cover, she begins to draw—delicate violets,
towering sunflowers, twining vines, and a few small bees
humming along the edges. Her hand moves with purpose,
each stroke a spell of care and creativity.

    At last, in the center of it all, she writes her name
in a soft, graceful script, *"sunshine."* The binder is no longer
just a collection—it's a garden in itself, a promise held
between pages. She holds it close to her chest, feeling
warmth bloom within her, a quiet affirmation that the
world can be messy and beautiful all at once.

I have to let go of this heavy vine,
the belief that it's my burden to carry everyone,
to be the roots that hold them steady—
because it's not my duty,
and the soil I've tilled can't bloom under such weight.

It's time to focus on the garden of *me*,
tend to the flowers I've neglected—
my heart, my soul, my mind—
before I can nurture others.
For in this sacred plot,
I must plant the seeds of self-love,
water them with patience,
and watch them grow strong and wild.

My children and my husband,
they are my sun and rain,
and together we'll cultivate a lush, vibrant garden—
where love blooms in every corner,
and we'll harvest peace from the soil we share.
We'll make a home of growth,
where each root is nourished,
and each bloom is cherished.

*"Am I doing enough?"*
*"Am I doing too much?"*
These questions swirl within me,
like a storm gathering on the horizon,
clouds heavy with doubt,
the winds of insecurity whipping through my thoughts.

I feel it rise,
a fiery dragon,
breathing flames of fear—
will they stay, or have I already burned the bridge?
*"Did I speak too soon?"*
*"Did I open my heart too wide, too fast?"*
I am caught in the tide—
too little, or too much—
never finding the shore.

But somewhere,
beneath the turmoil,
I sense the quiet pulse of nature—
a river flowing, finding its course,
neither rushing nor slowing,
but flowing steadily,
trusting the current.

One day,
I'll rest like the trees,
roots deep,
branches free.
No longer questioning every leaf I shed,
every storm I weather.
For I'll know
I am enough—
balanced between the earth and the sky,
living in harmony with my own rhythms.

It is not your fault—
the soil you were given was laced with weeds,
roots tangled in places they never belonged.
You did not plant them,
yet they grew, unbidden, unwelcome.

But now, with steady hands and tender care,
you hold the power to choose.
Will you let the weeds take over,
twisting, choking, claiming all the space?
Or will you pull them, one by one,
clear the earth,
and plant something softer, something strong,
something that blooms with almost every season?

Growth is yours to nurture.
*Your garden, your choice.*

*"But your home is so nice,"*
they would say, eyes tracing
the polished floors, the picture frames,
the walls that never spoke.
And I'd force a smile,
swallowing the truth like a bitter seed.
You don't know what happens
behind closed doors,
where silence is a fragile thread,
where every step is measured,
every breath, a calculation.

Is today a good day or a storm brewing?
Is his voice a whisper or a distant thunder?
Will he rage about the world,
or about the ghosts of his own failures?
Will I be one of them?
Little Lissa thought,
*"If his life is a failure, then what does that make me?"*
So she became more, did more,
much more than a child should.

A sapling bending under the weight of a forest,
a seedling forced to bloom before its time,
roots tangled in fear,
stretching toward approval like sunlight.

But a child is not meant
to be a caretaker of their parent's wounds,
to be the hands that patch together
a broken man's spirit.
A child should be free
to run barefoot in wild meadows,
to chase dreams, not shadows.
And now, I let myself run.

Dear self,
I long to be a sunlit soul,
radiant, casting warmth in every step,
spreading joy like golden rays,
simply by being.

I dream of feeling at home in my own skin,
to bask in the quiet peace of my existence,
where happiness blooms, not from reasons,
but from the pure essence of *just being*.

I yearn to stand in harmony with myself,
like a tree deeply rooted in its truth,
its branches swaying in alignment with the breeze,
finding my way back to the heart of who I am.

I know I'm walking the right path,
one step at a time,
as the earth heals beneath my feet,
and the sun guides my every move.

My father did support me, yes,
But it was more like a storm—
fierce, unpredictable,
never steady like the earth beneath me.
His love, though there,
was tangled in control,
like vines choking a fragile bloom.

He spoke good things,
but silence screamed louder—
the words left unspoken
hung in the air,
thicker than fog on an autumn morning.
I learned to read between the lines,
like tracing the cracks in a dry riverbed,
each one a sign of what was missing.

When his voice rose like thunder,
his eyes stormed with disappointment,
and in that heavy silence,
the weight of his gaze was enough to break me,
like a leaf too delicate for the harsh wind.
Then came the punishment—
to take my favorite toys away,
until the roots of my soul learned the lesson,
until I behaved.

It's not that he didn't care,
not that he wasn't trying,
but his best,
like a drought-stricken field,
was all he could give—
and it was the hardest kind of love.
His love, like the sun hiding behind clouds,
was there,

but I could never feel its warmth.

But I have learned—
like a tree that grows through cracked earth,
I will find my own sunlight,
reach past the shadows,
and let my roots grow strong,
untangled by the past.

The world hums softly outside,
the car's tires whispering across the road,
and we—carefree—giggle in the backseat,
kicking our feet,
dancing with the wind that teases through the cracks in the
windows.

Then, a sudden halt.
The engine's purr fades into silence,
a door swings open,
then slams shut.
Another door opens,
and his voice, like thunder over a summer field,
roars, *"Stop kicking or get out of the car!"*
And we, like flowers wilting under harsh sunlight,
stop, bubbles of laughter caught in our throats.

We sit, still as the night,
staring out at the passing world,
our imaginations soaring like birds,
painting dreams of what could be,
far from the storm we knew.

And yet, the car halts again,
my sister, behind him,
the one who kicked his seat,
lifted from her place in the back
like a fallen leaf tossed by the wind.
I screamed, a cry that rang out,
a plea to the universe that fell on deaf ears,
and my mother's voice joined mine,
a chorus of helplessness.

But the road was unyielding,
the earth indifferent.

he left her there,
alone on the side of the road,
the distance between us growing like a canyon.
And when he returned,
her tears like rainfall that soaked the earth,
he spoke in a voice like cracking branches:
*"Have you learned your lesson now, huh?"*

It's not the first time you've left—
drifting like a storm-torn leaf,
only to return when the wind calls you back.

But the damage lingers,
fractured stems, petals bruised,
a garden I must tend alone.

I can't let you in again,
not when I am still gathering
the pieces of what you shattered.

So this time, I'm the one leaving,
planting new roots where you can't reach.
Please don't hate me—
but this soil can no longer hold your storms.

No one talks about
how healing can feel like fire
before it feels like peace.
The anger isn't a setback—
it's proof that something inside you
is waking, stirring,
stretching toward the sun
after years of being buried in the dark.

Anger is the body's way of saying,
*"This wasn't okay."*
Let yourself listen.

You're not moving backward.
You're unraveling roots that never belonged,
clearing space for something new to grow.
Of course it hurts.
Of course it's messy.
But this is healing, too.

Let yourself feel it—
the past will loosen its grip,
but only if you stop running from it.

This won't break you.
It's breaking you open.
Like a seed splitting apart,
its tiny green tendrils pushing through the soil,
reaching for light.

And one day,
when you least expect it,
you'll look back and see—
you didn't just heal.
You bloomed.

No one fakes the weight of the storm,
the roots struggling beneath the soil,
the way shadows stretch too long in winter.

No—
they only try to fake the sunshine,
paint their petals bright,
stand tall despite the wind,
because saying *"I'm not okay"*
feels heavier than silence.

They don't want to be a burden,
don't want their trembling leaves to show,
so they tuck their pain beneath the surface,
even as they wither inside.

But even the strongest tree needs rain.
Even the wildflowers lean toward the light.
And no one should have to bloom alone.

I will never be the storm you were,
never let thunder rattle their small hearts,
never let love feel like something to be earned.

No—
I will be the sun on their skin,
the gentle rain that soothes,
the steady roots beneath their feet.

I will shower them in love,
wrap them in warmth,
fill their days with laughter,
with arms that never push away,
words that never wound.

I will tell them daily—
*You are enough.*
*You are loved.*

Because some things should never be a question.

Just hug me—
that's all I need.
Wrap me in your warmth,
like sunlight cradling petals at dawn.

In your arms,
I am safe,
sheltered from the storm,
steady as ancient roots in the earth.

I breathe you in—
your scent, like wildflowers after rain,
soft, familiar, full of life.

You have always been my harbor,
my quiet in the chaos,
my refuge when the winds howled too strong.

I love you—
like the trees love the sky,
like the rivers love the sea.
So please, never let me go.

*this poem was written to my husband and my kids <3

Save yourself—
love is a storm, and I know its wrath too well.
You've never felt waves this wild, this unforgiving.
So go—
before the sea pulls you under.

I learned young—
sink or swim, no in-between,
but you can't even bring yourself
to step into the water.
So save yourself.

If you're drowning—
in doubt,
self-hate,
the weight of yes when you mean no,
let the tide pull you somewhere safe.

As for me—
I will choose the shore,
I will plant my feet in solid ground,
I will let the saltwater cleanse me.
You can live your truth.
I will outgrow the ache of your absence.

It's clear now—
I never needed you.
That's okay.
Drift away.

*this poem was inspired by the song 'Save Yourself - Japanese Version'
from ONE OK ROCK.*

I want to teach my children
how to nurture soft roots,
how to cradle the earth in their hands
and whisper life into tiny seeds.

In our garden, mistakes are welcome—
if little hands pluck a plant too soon,
we'll press new seeds into the soil,
watch patience take shape in green.

Their laughter rings like wind chimes,
their curiosity, a gentle rain,
their joy, the sun that warms my soul.

And more than anything,
I want them to know—
this garden is more than soil and stems,
it's a lesson in love, in care,
in how to grow something beautiful,
inside and out.

*this poem was inspired by my kids and written for them <3

Like a steadfast sun, ever-waiting,
shrouded by clouds, soft and grating,
its golden fingers yearn to break free,
through whispers of sky's tapestry.

The clouds may linger, heavy and vast,
but none outlast the sun's bright cast.
Its warm embrace will find your skin,
inviting light and life within.

No matter how fogged your path may seem,
spring's tender hues will grace your dream.
So trust, as shadows stretch and wane,
the sun's embrace will shine again.

Maybe one morning, soft as the sigh
of autumn trees releasing their gold,
I will learn to let go, as they do—
whispering goodbye to their leaves,
giving them back to earth's embrace.

The wind will carry them—
a tender hush, as winter calls them home.
Though their branches stand bare,
they cradle the promise of spring—
a secret vow wrapped in frost,
a hope that knows no season.

And perhaps, in the quiet ache of endings,
I too will find the healing touch of change—
in the way even dying things weep,
only to rise again, reborn in time,
their roots still grounded,
and the beauty of their journey unfolding.

The rain taps gently on the leaves and pavement,
wrapping the world in a whisper of wet earth,
a scent that lingers, soft and satisfying—
it is everything.

The air, fresh with dew, hangs thick with mist,
blurring the horizon, where the distance fades,
and droplets of water kiss the skin,
awakening something deep, something alive.

Bare trees and bushes stand like silent ghosts,
their silhouettes hazy, almost forgotten in the fog.
And then, the sun—
it breaks through, a gentle promise,
its first warm rays, tender as a lover's touch,
grace the mist, and in that light,
when it meets your eye, you know—
you are loved.

It is magic,
and this season is a favorite song
the earth sings to me.

My sweet, soft child,
you did not deserve the storm,
the cold winds,
the weight of things too heavy for your small hands.

Come here—
let me wrap you in sunlight,
in the scent of wildflowers,
in the softness of moss beneath bare feet.

Let me hold you close,
rock you like the ocean rocks the shore,
whisper to you like the wind through the trees—
you are safe now.

Everything will be okay.
I promise.

No love—
it hollowed me like a canyon,
carving echoes where warmth should have been.

They say I love too deeply,
pour too much from hands that tremble with longing,
but how can I not?
When the drought has known only thirst,
does it not crave the rain?

I give, not from abundance, but ache—
a fire yearning to soften its own burn,
a river seeking to quench the barren earth.

For what I was never shown,
I long to plant in others,
to prove, through love,
that something beautiful can still grow.

I will never forget you.
You are the whisper of every wave,
the soft pulse of moonlit tides,
a breath that mingles with the sea's sigh.
You live with me, always—
a quiet current that courses through my veins,
carried in the depths of my soul,
a love too vast to be lost.

Each ripple echoes your presence,
a rhythm that beats in time with my heart,
woven into the fabric of sky and sea,
reminding me that what we lose
is never truly gone—
it only changes shape,
flowing beneath the surface
of all that remains.

Some days,
it feels as though the seed you planted
will never break through the darkness.
The soil feels heavy,
the light impossibly far away.

But don't worry—
give it time.

With tender care,
a whisper of water,
and the warmth of love,
that seed will stir beneath the surface.
It will push, ever so gently,
breaking through the tiny barrier of earth,
reaching toward the sun,
stretching its weary stem skyward.

And there it will stand—
a fragile sprout, trembling but alive,
a quiet miracle of your nurture,
ready to grow stronger,
ready to thrive.

Inside, there is life—
a wild garden waiting to bloom.
Her soul hums with color,
vivid and untamed,
roots stretching toward the sun.

But she clings to the withered leaves,
the careful facade,
afraid that if she lets go,
she will crumble like autumn's last breath.

Yet the earth knows her truth.
Her body remembers—
she was never meant to shrink,
only to grow.

I walk alone through quiet streets,
the city asleep, wrapped in silence.
The full moon spills silver light,
soft against my weary face.

The roads are empty,
no footsteps, no voices—
only the whisper of the wind
guiding me forward.

But the sky is alive—
stars flicker like distant lanterns,
and the moon, ever watchful,
casts a glow upon my path.

In their quiet radiance,
I find company.
In their light,
I am never truly alone.

I know the storms have been relentless,
winds howling, roots shaken,
but please believe me when I say—
there is still light, still warmth,
still hands reaching for yours.

Somewhere, beneath the soil of sorrow,
seeds of love are waiting to bloom.
There are people in this world
who will see you as you are,
who will cherish every scar,
who will walk beside you through every season.

Don't give up hope.
Like the river finds the sea,
like the sun finds the dawn,
you will find them,
and they will find you.

*"This is not good enough,"*
I'd say, crumpling the page,
like a leaf pressed too hard,
its edges torn by my own doubts.
*"I'm not as good as my friend,"*
and the joy of creation withers,
like a flower that doesn't bloom.

I'd show my mother the petals of my art—
she would smile,
tell me she was proud,
but my father's indifference felt like a storm cloud,
dimming the colors I once trusted.
I practiced, like a gardener tending a plot,
but the soil felt barren,
until I thought, *"there's no point,"*
and let my hands fall still.

I stopped planting dreams,
telling myself I'd never sprout,
never rise like a seed toward the sun.
I'd tell myself no one would listen,
that my voice would be lost in the wind,
a breeze no one would notice.

But even the quietest seed,
buried in the dark,
knows it is meant to grow.
And the rain will come,
washing away doubts,
and soon, the garden will bloom again.

There is something beautiful
in the art of breaking—
tears falling like shattered glass,
each drop a mirror of the past.

In the fragments scattered on the floor,
a quiet promise: you'll be whole once more.

Piece by piece, you gather what's lost,
rebuilding yourself, no matter the cost.

And in the cracks, something new will shine,
a version of you, both tender and devine.

There is beauty in the breaking—
and in discovering yourself anew.

Let the rain wash away my pain,
let each drop fall like whispered grace,
a cascade of tears upon my skin,
cleansing the scars that lie within.

Let it transform me, soft and slow,
a healing touch from skies below.

Let the storm reshape my soul,
until I am whole, reborn, and whole again.

Dear little one,
you gave your all,
tending to others' gardens
when your hands were already weary,
when you should have tended your own.
And so, it withered—
quiet and forgotten.

But fear not, sweet soul.
The earth remembers how to heal.
You can always re-grow.

With love as sunlight,
and water as forgiveness,
your garden will bloom again—
lush, vibrant, alive.

And when its petals open wide,
when colors burst from every corner,
only then,
may you reach out to water another's garden,
freely, without losing your own.

Remember this, little one:
you cannot give
what you do not nurture.

How many times were you told
you were not enough,
that you'd never reach the heights you dreamed?
Those words—sharp as thorns—
took root, didn't they?

But listen.
Feel the wind as it stirs around you,
gentle and unyielding.
Let it carry those heavy words away,
scattering them like brittle leaves,
far from your heart.

Now, plant new seeds instead.
Whisper to yourself:
*"I am strong.
I can grow.
I can reach the sky."*

Don't let the shadows of others' doubts
or the echoes of your own fears
keep you rooted in place.
Stretch toward the sun,
even when it feels uncertain,
even when the horizon feels so far away.

Try something new—
something that makes your heart race.
Because you can do it.
Like a tree breaking through stone,
you can rise.
If you truly want it,
you can bloom.

I know you long for a happy ending,
a tale where everyone blooms,
even at the cost of your own roots,
but that, dear soul, is not where healing begins.

Some stories are like wilted flowers—
their petals, once vibrant, now faded,
leaving an unsettling ache within you.
There are chapters that do not fit into your garden,
stories that cannot be woven into the fabric of your peace.

And it's okay to set that book down,
to close its pages without the neatness of closure,
for some endings are not meant to be rewritten,
just as a tree must shed its leaves
to grow stronger with the seasons.

Let go of what no longer serves you,
and in that stillness, you will find
a new chapter,
where your heart can bloom freely,
nurtured by the soil of your own worth.

For a change—
pause.
Stop being the one who always stirs the waters,
who rows the boat upstream,
against the current of your own needs.

Breathe in the air,
let it fill your lungs like fresh rain,
feel the earth beneath your feet,
rooted in stillness.

Sit back, and watch.
Let the ship sail on its course,
if it sinks, let it.
Sometimes, the river knows better
than the hand that tries to steer it.

In the quiet, observe—
the flow of the world,
the release of effort,
and in that surrender,
find the strength to rise again,
like a tree after the storm.

For many years,
I buried my feelings deep—
like seeds in soil,
afraid to let them sprout.

I thought no one would understand,
that I was too broken to be heard,
but in the quiet of the forest,
I've learned something precious:
most people are like trees—
rooted in their own struggles,
yet reaching for the same sunlight,
fighting the same storms.

You'd be surprised how many share the same wounds,
how many have felt the ache of a bruised heart,
it's sad, yes,
but in that shared grief,
there is a gentle strength.
A strength in speaking your truth,
in letting the wind carry away your fears,
in letting the rain wash away the pain.

When you speak,
it's like a wildflower breaking through the earth—
bringing light to the darkness,
creating space for healing to bloom.

So, please—
don't be afraid to ask for help,
just like the trees lean on each other in the storm,
we can lean on one another,
and grow stronger together.

I grew up too fast,
like a seed forced to sprout in winter,
pushing through frozen ground
to reach a sun that never warmed me.

I became an adult
before my hands had even learned
the softness of childhood.
Instead of laughter,
I walked barefoot on broken glass,
patched up fires I never set,
held together a home that crumbled in my hands.

Too young to understand,
too small to carry your weight,
I became the "fixer"
while losing myself,
roots tangled in soil
that was never mine to tend.

But seasons change.
Now, I gather my own light,
growing beyond the past,
reclaiming the childhood
that still lingers in the wind,
waiting for me to run freely at last.

We cry—
tears pooling like rainclouds too heavy to hold.
Because if we speak of this storm inside,
we are met with thunder,
with silence,
with indifference.

If we demand change,
our roots are ripped from the earth,
our light taken away.
So, we fall in line—
dammed rivers, holding back the flood,
swallowing the tide.

But this is not love.
This is not how things should be.

We cry—
because resentment cracks like dry earth,
because anger burns like wildfire,
because we once thought you were shelter,
but you were only the storm.

Still, the rain will come,
not to drown us,
but to cleanse—
to break the dam,
to let something new grow.

As a child, in a world that never felt safe,
you learned to hold the cracks together,
piece by fragile piece,
trying to make sense of what was broken,
carrying a weight that should never have been yours.

But now, dear soul,
you can lay it down.
Feel the burden lift,
like leaves slipping from the branches in autumn,
carried gently on a summer breeze.

Close your eyes,
let the wind sweep through you,
soft and warm,
whispering of freedom, of healing.
You don't need to carry it anymore.

Release it to the sky,
where it can drift beyond the horizon,
and feel the earth beneath your feet,
solid, steady,
ready to hold you as you grow anew.

You cannot change the past—
its stones are set,
its rivers have already run their course.
But the future?
The future is soft clay,
wet with possibility,
waiting in your hands.

It's okay if your first shape cracks,
if the lines aren't smooth,
or the edges crumble.
You can reshape it,
dip your fingers in the water of patience,
and build again.

Like the seeds you plant in spring,
it takes time, care, and courage.
Each sunrise gives you a fresh start,
each breath, a second chance.
And so, dear soul,
you shape tomorrow with quiet persistence,
every single day.

It's spring—the kind of spring where the air hums with newness, and the birds practice their brightest tunes, shaking off winter with each joyful note. Sunshine breathes it all in, feeling the lightness settle on her skin, like a soft veil. The days are longer now, and the warmth seeps into the earth, coaxing the soil to awaken. It's the perfect day to clear out the remnants of winter and prepare the garden for its highest potential.

Sunshine begins by gently pulling away the old, weary plants from the garden beds, roots trailing like forgotten stories. She tosses them into the organic bin, where they'll transform into compost—rich, dark, and full of promise. As she works, the scent of damp soil fills the air, earthy and grounding. The garden hums in quiet approval. Next, she plunges her hands into the soil, turning it over with practiced care, mixing in fertilizer like a secret ingredient in a beloved recipe. She layers fresh, airy soil on top, patting it gently, as if tucking in a child for the night. There's something sacred in this preparation, a quiet ritual that sings of hope and growth.

As the sun climbs to its highest point, she hauls out the hose, attaching the high-pressure cleaner and aiming it at the greenhouse. The spray arches through the sunlight, droplets like tiny prisms scattering rainbows across the grass. She uses a gentle, biodegradable soap, mindful of the creatures who call the garden home. With a soft-bristled brush, she scrubs away the winter grime, whispering apologies to the spiders who skitter to safer corners.

Inside and out, she works, until the glass gleams like a jewel, framing the world in crystalline light.

Sweaty and a little breathless, she steps back to admire her work, wiping her forehead with a dirt-smudged hand. The greenhouse glows, catching the sun's rays and holding them like a treasure chest of warmth. She heads inside to tend to the garden beds, where winter's vegetables still cling to their places. Though some leaves have grown bitter with age, the flowers they've sprouted hint at the seeds to come—a gift from one season to the next. Sunshine leaves them be, respecting the cycle of life. She knows the sourness of today might give way to sweetness tomorrow. Sighing, she sits down in the greenhouse, feeling the sun kiss her shoulders through the spotless glass. A deep peace settles over her, the kind that only comes after hard, mindful work. In this place, surrounded by life in all its stages, she feels at home—rooted, like the garden itself.

You did your best.
like a tree bending in the storm,
you stood firm,
even when the winds howled
and the skies darkened.

You survived.
like the wildflowers that bloom
in the cracks of stone,
you found a way to rise,
even when the world seemed unkind.

And that's enough.
Let the sun kiss your face,
let the gentle rain cleanse your spirit.
You are here,
rooted and resilient,
and that is more than enough.

Be kind to yourself,
even when the weight of the world feels heavy.
I know it's hard,
and it's okay if you don't have the resources right now.
Like a seed in the dark soil,
you are still growing.
Patience, little one.
The rain will come,
the sunlight will find you again.

Time and nature are on our side—
the earth knows how to heal,
and so do we.
The roots stretch deep,
drawing strength from the quiet,
from the stillness between the storms.

We are strong,
you and I.
Remember this:
like the river that carves through mountains,
we may bend,
but we will never break.
we flow forward,
we rise again.

Imagine yourself as a tiny seed,
nestled deep beneath the earth,
waiting, resting,
holding quiet potential in the dark.

It doesn't matter how long you've lain dormant,
how many seasons have passed,
or how often you forgot to nurture yourself.

Because, like the seed,
you can sleep beneath the soil for years,
yet the moment you give yourself water,
the moment you offer yourself care,
you will stir, awaken, reach for the light.

So don't fret—
it is never too late.
The sun is still shining for you,
the rain is still willing to fall.
Show yourself kindness,
let your roots take hold,
and watch as the scars of your past
blossom into wildflowers,
soft, strong, and free.

Sink your hands deep into the soil,
feel the cool, damp earth embrace your fingers.
Let it cling beneath your nails—
there is no shame in the mess of growth.

Close your eyes, breathe it in—
the scent of renewal, of life waiting to bloom.
This soil holds endless possibilities,
a thousand seeds waiting for your touch,
a garden shaped by your own hands.

You decide what will grow here—
wildflowers that dance in the wind,
vines that climb toward the sun,
roots that hold steady through every storm.

So dig deep, plant with intention,
and watch as the earth gives back
all the love you pour into it.

This can't be us.
Not like this.
Let me turn back time,
rewind the seasons,
give you a chance to bloom,
to be the roots I never had.

I wanted you to be the sun,
warm and steady,
but you were always the winter—
distant, fading, too cold to hold.

I don't want to say goodbye,
but I know now,
this is a seed that will never sprout.

So I will let you wither,
fall like autumn leaves,
and drift away with the wind.

And I—
I will plant something new.

*this poem was inspired by the song 'This Can't Be Us' from ONE OK
ROCK.*

I guess I never mattered,
or why else would you
cast me aside like a wilted bouquet,
petals bruised, stem snapped,
left to wither without a second glance?

I guess I never mattered,
or why else would our words
shrink down to nothing,
except for the one thing
I begged not to say?

But I am not just the remnants
of what you discarded.
I will gather these broken petals,
press them into soil rich with lessons,
let the rain mend what you tried to uproot.

And soon, a garden will rise—
wild, untamed, full of color,
full of life.

Because I do matter.
I matter to me.

I want to be unapologetically me,
but how can I,
when I don't even know who that is?

When I look in the mirror,
I see the echoes of storms I've weathered,
the scars left behind like fallen branches,
the pain like roots tangled deep.

But I also see love—
soft as petals unfolding at dawn,
resilient as ivy climbing toward the sun.

And these eyes—
they have seen darkness,
but they have also glimpsed the light.

I may not know myself now,
but like a river finding its course,
like a seed remembering the sun,
I will find my way back again.

Sometimes I wonder—*was any of it real?*
You were kind, soft as spring rain,
until the storm rolled in,
until your words turned to thorns,
and I was left bleeding.

Yes, there were good times, bright moments,
but now I sift through the ashes,
trying to decide if they were warmth or wildfire.
Were you sincere, or just a master of illusion?
I could forgive if I knew the truth,
but something in my roots tells me otherwise.

I have to remember the storm,
the way you tore through me like a hurricane,
so I don't run back,
so I don't mistake destruction for home.

You were supposed to be my shelter,
but instead, you uprooted me,
tossed me into an unfamiliar forest,
where the path is dark and unknown.

But I will walk it anyway.
I will carve my own way through the trees,
find the light that filters through the branches,
let my roots take hold in new, fertile ground.

And one day, I will emerge—
not lost, not broken,
but stronger, wilder,
finally free.

I want to plant smiles like wildflowers,
scatter light in the darkest corners,
tell them they matter,
that they are radiant,
that they are enough—
just as they are.

I want to give what I never received,
water others with the kindness
my own roots thirsted for as a child.
Every word I offer them—
gentle, warm, full of love—
is a seed I must also plant within myself.

Because my inner child still listens,
still waits,
still deserves to bloom.

No love—
it hollowed me out,
carved an emptiness I carry still,
taught me just how vital love is,
like sunlight to a starving seed.

They say I love too deeply,
give too much,
that my hands spill over
with a desperate touch.
But how can I not,
when all I crave
is to kindle the warmth
I was once denied by the fire?

I give, not from abundance,
but from drought—
a thirst to flood the cracks,
to soften the hardened earth within.

For what I was never shown,
I yearn to give—
love like rain,
gentle, endless,
turning barren soil
into bloom.

Not many really knows this,
but I have danced with the dark,
suicidal thoughts weaving in and out,
like tides that refuse to recede.

For years, they came and went,
whispering, waiting—
until one day, I had a plan.
My search history bears witness,
silent proof of how ready I was
to say goodbye to it all.

I sat with the weight of it,
let it settle into my bones,
until the phone rang—
a voice pulling me back to shore,
a thread of light in the thick of it all.

And in that moment,
I knew—
I didn't want to die,
I just wanted the pain to stop.

So I made a new plan.
I called my doctor.
I chose to protect myself.
To sever the ties that strangled me,
no matter how selfish they said it was.

Because survival is not selfish.
Because I deserve to bloom.


*this poem was written to a person who saved my life.*

I've grown used to playing pretend,
wearing a smile like a mask of spun gold,
so seamless, so practiced,
no one notices the fractures beneath.

But inside, I am unraveling,
a quiet storm, a bird in a gilded cage,
wings folded, voice silenced,
waiting—aching—to be seen.

Please,
unlatch the door,
let the wind carry me beyond the weight of silence,
let me rise with the sun,
let me unfurl my wings,
and finally, finally,
soar.

The only hands that will never drop you
are your own.
You are the roots that steady you,
the sky that holds your dreams.
You are your own best friend.

Not everything is meant to be mended—
some things must fall like autumn leaves,
be carried away like rivers to the sea.
Letting go is not loss;
it is making space to bloom again.

Trust yourself.
Like the sun that rises without doubt,
like the tide that knows when to retreat.
Some things cannot be fixed—
but you, love,
you are not broken.

You must plant seeds of connection,
tend to the roots of your relationships—
Nurture those who nourish you,
like sunlight to the leaves,
and cool water to the soil.

True families are not born of blood—
they are grown, slowly,
like vines twisting together,
strengthened through love,
pruned through understanding.

It's the bond that heals,
the shared moments that blossom,
and the warmth that holds you—
These are the ties that truly matter.
Genetics are just the soil;
love is what makes us bloom.

I wear my laughter like sunlight,
bright, warm—
a trick of the light to keep the shadows at bay.
Jokes bubble up like a river's song,
washing over the ache,
but only for a moment.

Don't be fooled by the girl who glows—
underneath, she has cracked like dry earth in a drought,
hurt herself to silence the storm,
tried to vanish with the tide.

Still, I laugh.
Because sometimes, humor feels like the only raft
on an ocean too deep,
too dark.

But even the strongest currents find the shore,
even the heaviest clouds break for light.
And I am learning—
that I don't have to drown in silence
to make the pain go away.

Be patient,
like the seed nestled beneath the earth,
waiting for the sun's embrace.

Breathe—
let the wind carry away your worries,
let the rain soften the soil around you.

Growth takes time,
petals don't unfurl in a day,
roots don't anchor overnight.

But you will bloom,
when the season is right,
when your heart is ready.

Trust the process.
You'll get there.

For the first time,
I'm allowing myself to dream—
not of grandeur, not of fame,
but of roots sinking deep
into someone else's soul,
half a world away,
finding shelter in my words.

I don't need to make it big
or stand on stages soaked in light—
I just want to plant a seed
in someone's heart,
one that blooms with recognition,
a tiny wildflower growing
from a crack in their heavy concrete.

If they read my story,
and see themselves reflected
like sunlight on a quiet river,
if they feel a little less alone,
a little more seen—
then I've done enough.
That's all I want.
The rest doesn't matter to me.

Vase shattered on the floor,
water pooling like unshed tears.
Scattered petals whisper loss,
fragile remnants of something once whole.

I stand in the wreckage,
bare feet among the broken pieces,
trapped in a storm of memory.

But even shattered things find new form—
water seeps into the earth,
petals return to the soil,
and from the wreckage,
something new will bloom.

I'm broken—who's gonna mend me?
Splintered like a fallen branch,
scattered like autumn leaves in the wind.

Memories choke like tangled vines,
pulling me back, pulling me under.
Every time I try to mend, I burn,
like wildfire licking at my edges,
turning hope to ash.

But even in ruin, seeds remain.
Even in darkness, roots reach deeper.
So I cry for help—
not to be fixed,
but to be planted anew.

*this poem was inspired by the song 'Tiny Pieces' from ONE OK ROCK.*

Most of your life
is spent inside your own head,
so why not make it a garden—
a place where sunlight lingers,
where thoughts bloom soft as wildflowers,
where the wind hums lullabies
through the swaying green vines?

Plant kindness in the soil of your mind.
Let laughter flow like a river,
cool and endless.
Scatter butterflies in the corners,
whispering hope with every flutter.

Make it a place to rest,
not a place to run from.
A home, not a battleground.
A sanctuary where you can breathe,
where you can finally be.

I was just a seed,
trying to make sense of the soil,
you took and took,
drained my roots,
leaving me to wither in your shadow.

But even in the dark,
I found my own sunlight—
I learned to fight for myself,
to push through cracked earth
and stretch toward the sky,
no longer waiting for someone to water me.

I will grow,
even without your love,
like wildflowers breaking through stone,
fighting for my place in this world.

Buried deep,
suffocating in the weight of the earth,
I thought the only way out
was to disappear into the roots.

No light. No air. Just silence.

But then—
a gentle rain, soft hands,
someone whispered my name in the dark,
poured water over my fragile soul,
nurtured me, cradled me in warmth.

Slowly, tenderly,
I unfurled,
learning to love the light again.

He stayed—
like the steady moon,
illuminating my path,
while I, the sun,
learned to rise once more.

*this poem was written for my husband <3*

I have trouble opening up—
like a flower that closes at dusk,
guarding its petals against the night,
I tread lightly, wary of the cold.
Trust doesn't come easily—
I've been scorched by too many summers,
left wilted and dry,
so I gauge and assess,
wondering, *"will this sun bring warmth or burn?"*

It's like my mind is always in fight or flight,
roots tangled, branches trembling in the wind.
To protect myself, I stay quiet—
a listener in the forest,
waiting to know if the footsteps approaching
mean harm or kindness.

But sometimes, the right people come—
gentle as rain, steady as oak,
who see the whole garden of me—
not just the weeds of hurt or the scars of drought,
but the wildflowers, too—
the vibrant, untamed, beautiful me.
When you find those souls,
let them in, water them with gratitude—
for they, too, might have known storms,
and still chose to bloom.

To find love and friendship,
you must let your heart crack open,
risk the pain to feel the sun,
and though it might be scary—
you'll be okay.
You'll grow.
And it will be worth it.

I know I speak of gardens often,
of roots stretching deep,
of wildflowers dancing in the wind.

But I know—
not everyone has soil to call their own,
not everyone has a patch of earth to plant in.

Still, don't let that stop you.
No one ever said a garden
must live outside.

Let it bloom within you—
a windowsill bursting with green,
a single flower pressed between book pages,
a dream nurtured in the quiet corners of your heart.

Because healing is not about where you plant,
but how you let yourself grow.

I have mourned the childhood
I never had—
the warmth that never reached me,
the gentle words I never heard,
the safety I never knew.

But I will not let the past
write my children's story.

Like sunlight breaking through dense branches,
I will carve a path of love,
of laughter that echoes like wind in the trees,
of hands held tight,
of voices soft with understanding.

I will give them the warmth I longed for,
the kindness I craved,
the childhood I deserved.

I cannot rewrite my own past,
but I can plant new seeds—
and make sure they grow wild and free.

They say, *"be grateful,
your pain made you stronger."*
Well, fuck them.
I don't feel strong at all.
I feel like a brittle wildflower,
wilting beneath the weight of winter,
roots tangled in frost,
thirsting for warmth that never came.

My trauma didn't shape me into steel—
it left fractures in my foundation,
ghosts in my breath,
patterns I must unlearn,
fears I must untangle,
a mind I must rewire,
just to call this place home again.

Strength was never in the suffering—
it's in the choice to heal,
to press my palms into the earth,
turn my face toward the light,
and begin again.

I'm not as fine as I pretend,
downplaying wounds that never mend.
Like leaves that hide a weathered tree,
I mask the hurt no one can see.

What good is silence in disguise,
but choking roots with quiet lies?
A garden growing thorns instead—
wild vines of pain inside my head.

Still, I don't dare let sorrow show—
I fear the storm they'll never know.
But every seed of truth I hide
takes root and grows, unbloomed, inside.

Perhaps one day I'll let them see
the wildflowers blooming in me—
roots strong from all the storms I've braved,
no longer scared to be unscathed.

Drowning sorrow, sip by sip,
like rain that overflows the lip
of weary earth, too soaked to hold—
a flood that drowns the roots in mold.

The world blurs, shadows fade,
as twilight swallows light unmade.
Troubles drift like autumn leaves,
carried by the wind that grieves—
gone, for now, not mine to claim,
until dawn calls me by my name.

But morning breaks through hazy dreams,
sunlight spills in golden streams.
Roots breathe deep, their thirst fulfilled—
a promise that the earth is healed.

Healing doesn't come so fast—
storms subside, but rains still last.
Still, I hope for brighter skies,
where sorrow's roots can't grip or rise.

My head drifts high among the clouds,
wandering through dreams unbound—
what I could have been, what I should have known,
the endless paths I left unsown.

Branches reach where I couldn't go,
roots tangled in the earth below.
All the ifs and all the whys
scatter like leaves beneath quiet skies.

I trace the stars with weary eyes,
mapping futures wrapped in lies.
In the end, it seems to be,
I'm still not at peace with me.

But one day, like the dawn that breaks
through foggy hills and mirrored lakes,
I'll find the light that sets me free—
and finally make peace with me.

Feelings are fleeting, or so they say—
but why does their weight refuse to stray?
Why can't I stand apart, observe,
like a lone tree bent by a gusting curve—
rooted, grounded, safe from harm,
whispering, *"this too will calm."*

*"It's just a storm; soon skies will clear,*
*and warmth will follow where clouds appear."*
Yet my mind betrays what I try to sell,
each word a wave that swells and swells.
I drown in tides of doubt unseen,
lost in the depths where hope has been.

But time, like rivers, shapes the stone—
softening edges once overthrown.
My feelings will lessen, find their flow,
and I'll speak kindly to the soul I know.
One day, I'll bloom beyond the rain,
and I hope that peace remains.

I long for the Earth to open wide,
to pull me in where shadows hide—
a place where roots embrace the deep,
and weary souls can finally sleep.

Let me vanish, leave no trace,
like falling leaves in autumn's grace.
Consumed by silence, lost in space,
where storms subside without a chase.

No whispers left, no memory drawn—
just buried deep, where night meets dawn.
But seeds that rest beneath the stone
one day will break the ground alone.

For even when the dark enfolds,
life finds a way, as soil holds
the promise of a bloom reborn—
a flower reaching toward the morn.

Speaking kindly to myself feels like an uphill climb—
scaling mountains carved from bitter years.
How do I turn the ashes of my past
into fields where wildflowers outlast
the frost that claimed my heart, once bold,
now brittle, left in winter's hold?

How do I nurture a heart long left cold,
when years of neglect have silenced my chime?
I've planted others where I couldn't grow—
roots tangled, twisted, left to overflow.
Lost in the shadows, who am I, truly?
a stranger in the mirror, a tale unruly—

But beneath the brambles, seeds remain,
waiting for light, for summer's rain.
Yet within the darkness, can I find my whole?
A garden reborn from fractured soil,
where flowers reach through cracks of pain—
and hope unfurls like dawn again.

I long to cradle my heart with care,
to tend to myself as I tend to others—
like flowers kissed by morning dew,
I wish to nurture the soul I know.

This stranger within, so harsh and unkind,
yearns for the softness I so freely find.
To wrap myself in the warmth I give,
to let my spirit finally live.

I wish to whisper sweet words in the night,
like winds that hum, soft and light.
To cradle my heart in gentle sound,
and let love grow from hallowed ground.

To believe in the kindness that dances in me—
like leaves that tremble on a blossoming tree,
can I learn to bloom, and set myself free—
to love who I am, to be whole, to be me?

Sometimes I wonder—
will I wander forever,
lost in the twisting corridors
of this endless maze
I call my mind?

Shadows whisper, walls constrict,
yet I feel a distant flicker,
a tender glow,
promising escape,
a freedom I've yet to know.

Perhaps not today, nor tomorrow,
but someday—
someday the darkness will break.
The light will spill like a rising sun,
pouring through cracks,
illuminating the path
to a world unbound.

And when that day arrives,
I'll breathe deep,
unshackle my soul,
and finally,
be free.

My mind is a treacherous sea—
waves towering, fierce currents that plea,
dragging me under,
its cold, unyielding embrace a weight—
a storm that swells within my fate.

The air grows thin;
each breath a fragile, fleeting win.
Each stroke a battle fought with fear,
pushing through waters, dark and clear.
Will I surface, gasping for light,
or sink into silence, swallowed by night?

The storm rages on, wild and deep—
yet, beneath the chaos, a promise sleeps.
Will this relentless swim be my last—
a broken shell upon the vast?
Or will I find a shoreline near,
where gentle waves calm the fear?

Perhaps the ocean, though harsh and wide,
holds the answers on the other side—
the tides will soften, and skies will clear,
healing winds will draw me near.
For even in the fiercest storm,
the sea, like life, can still transform.

Please, don't speak harshly to your mind,
for you become the seeds you plant and bind.
Words are the roots, thoughts the soil—
choose them with care, for they will toil.
You can rewrite your own tale,
I know it's hard, and the path is frail,
but no matter how long the road may wind,
trust, in time, you will find—

That healing isn't swift or sure,
but it is a bloom that will endure.
For, at last, my mind is filled with flowers,
soft petals stretching toward the hours—
through every season, rain or sun,
new growth, new light, a journey begun.

And for the first time, I am free,
a garden flourishing inside of me.
No longer the weeds of doubt take hold—
I am a meadow, wild and bold.
For the first time, I see the grace,
of learning to love this sacred space.

Earlier,
I said I was okay.
But the truth is,
I'm not.
There's a storm moving through me—
quiet,
heavy,
unseen.

Will you stay with me?
Not to fix,
not to speak—
just to be.

Like the moon stays with the tide,
like the roots stay with the earth,
hold me,
without asking me to bloom.
Just be the ground beneath me,
while I weather this.

We don't have to talk.
Your presence,
like soft rain on thirsty soil,
is enough.
Just stay.
While I slowly grow
through this silence.

It's so easy
to fight for my kids—
to stand strong like a tree,
roots deep, branches wide,
sheltering them
from every storm.

But I forget
that I'm still a kid, too—
a small, wildflower heart
beating inside me,
soft and curious,
needing protection,
needing love.

Just as I fight
for them—
shielding them, loving them,
with fierce, unwavering strength—
I need to fight
for that small voice within me,
for the little one
who still longs to be heard.

I will guard my joy
like a blooming garden—
water what grows,
and weed out what doesn't.
I will protect my peace
like a sacred forest—
only allowing in
what nurtures my soul.

So, little one,
I promise you this:

I'll fight for you, too.
I'll hold your hand
and walk gently
through the wild,
giving you room
to blossom
in your own time.

That is a promise
I give you now—
to love and protect you
like I do my own children,
because you deserve
to feel safe,
to feel loved,
to feel whole.

Sunshine has an assortment of seed trays, each a different
size, like a collection of tiny beds awaiting sleepy dreams.
In a morning wrapped in mist and dew, she ventures out to
the greenhouse, where the world feels softened around the
edges. A quiet magic lingers in the cool air, settling on the
glass like a whispered promise.

She pulls the box filled with seedling soil onto her
workbench. It's the kind meant for fragile beginnings—
low in fertilizer and nutrients, just enough to coax tiny
seeds awake. Sunshine mixes it with vermiculite and perlite,
letting the grains sift through her fingers, feeling the texture
change from dense to airy, heavy to light. Soil finds its way
under her nails, but she doesn't mind—she's always loved
the raw, earthy feeling of it.
As she mixes, a hum slips from her lips, a melody as soft as
dawn. When the seedling mix is just right—light, crumbly,
and full of potential—she fills four big trays, each a cradle
for botanical life. She makes sure every cell is brimful,
then gives each tray a gentle thump on the corner of the
garden bed, settling the soil like fluffing a pillow before
sleep.

Once the trays are on the ground, she fills her watering can,
letting the stream catch the morning light, scattering tiny
rainbows. She moistens the soil, careful not to drown it,
just enough to coax it into readiness. Then, one by one,
she lifts each tray, her fingers curling around her dibber
pen. With rhythmic precision, she pokes little nests into the

soil, each one waiting for a seed to rest inside.
Gently, she cradles the seed packets, each labeled with
a hand-drawn doodle and a name. Watermelon, cabbage,
tomatoes, and more—future feasts in small, humble forms.
One by one, she sprinkles the seeds into the soil's embrace,
murmuring soft encouragements as they disappear beneath
the surface. When all the trays are filled, she dusts a final,
thin layer of soil on top—a soft blanket tucking them in for
the night.
"Sleep tight, little ones," she whispers, leaning close as if
sharing a secret. With the spray bottle, she mists the surface,
gentle as a morning drizzle, careful not to disturb the seeds
from their cozy beds. She doesn't trust the watering can for
this part—one harsh splash, and the careful order would
unravel.

      Finally, she sets the trays on the greenhouse
shelves, each one labeled with a lovingly crafted sign.
Dusting off her hands, she steps back, feeling a calm settle
over her. The fog still holds the world in its hazy embrace
but the morning light peeks through, the greenhouse
glowing softly from within. Sunshine takes a deep breath,
soaking in the stillness, feeling complete and grounded.
A lovely morning indeed.

# the sprout

The seedling is fragile, yes—but within its delicate frame lies a vast and unyielding potential. It is small, trembling in the hush of dawn, yet instinctively reaching—toward the golden embrace of the sun, toward the nourishment that will awaken its slumbering strength. Light calls to it, whispers to it, promising life in every radiant beam.

   Yet, growth is a dance of balance. Too much water, and the soil sours, heavy with decay; too little, and the earth cracks, brittle and unforgiving. But when the elements align just so—when warmth kisses the soil and moisture cradles the roots in perfect harmony—
the seedling stirs. It unfurls, pressing against the weight of the earth, breaking through with quiet determination, seeking purpose in the open air.
I love to watch them—these tiny green souls—bearing their first set of leaves, the cotyledons that once lay curled in darkness, now trembling in the light. I marvel at their soft resilience, how they stretch skyward with fearless hunger. How delicate they seem, yet how steadfast they stand in the face of each passing breeze. I nourish them, whisper to them, guide them gently into their next chapter.

And from these small sprouts, we, too, can learn.
Growth is not a race but a steady, patient unfurling.
We must take our time, sending our roots deep into the earth, anchoring ourselves before we reach for the sky.
Even when planted in barren or unkind soil, even when scarred by storms, we can still sprout. We can still heal.
No matter the weight of our past, no matter the wounds we carry, the light is always there, waiting for us to rise toward it once more. It is never too late.
One day, the seedling will outgrow the confines of its first home. Its roots, once so small and contained, will push

against the edges of the pot, yearning for space, for freedom.
And that will be the moment to transplant it—to lift it
with gentle, loving hands, to place it somewhere vast and
open, where it can stretch, where it can breathe, where it
can bloom.

Do this with tenderness. Smile as you press new
soil around its base, as you water it with care.
Know that your hands are the hands of the earth itself,
shaping, supporting, guiding. For though the seedling is
fragile, with love and patience, it will not just survive—
it will thrive. And so will you.

It's summer, and the heat drapes itself over the garden like a heavy, sun-soaked quilt. Sunshine steps outside in a tank top and shorts, her skin kissed golden by the sun. A pang of discomfort flickers through her mind as she glances down at her brown skin, tracing the scars that map her body like winding rivers. She takes a breath, deep and steady, letting the warmth sink in, reminding herself that her skin tells stories—of growth, of healing, of surviving.

She hums a tune—bright and carefree—and lets the melody guide her steps through the garden. The song bubbles up, lightening her spirit, until she's dancing as she waters each plant, her feet brushing against the soft, sun-warmed earth. Droplets glisten on leaves like tiny jewels, catching the sunlight and reflecting it back in playful flickers.

The smell of summer wraps around her—sweet blossoms, sun-dried grass, and a hint of earthiness from the soil. She moves from one patch to the next, tending to every flower and vegetable with equal care. It's an honor to witness their growth, knowing that some are annuals—bright and fleeting—while others are biennials, lingering longer, blooming twice to savor the world just a bit more.

Sunshine kneels to sniff a cluster of marigolds, their golden faces turned toward her like little suns. She trails her fingers over the soft petals of the cosmos, whispering encouragement. As she works, she feels the tension in her shoulders dissolve, replaced by the gentle hum of life around her. Butterflies dance lazily in the heavy air, and bees buzz with purpose, dipping in and out of blossoms like tiny alchemists.

The colors swirl around her—fiery reds, cool purples, and dazzling whites, each one vibrant against the rich green foliage. A giddy happiness wells up inside her, and for a moment, she pauses, breathing it all in, feeling rooted and free. Out here, in the embrace of her garden, she feels beautiful—not despite her scars, but because they are part of the wild, resilient tapestry of her life.

She could stay here for hours, cradled by the earth, wrapped in the garden's song. It's not just a space—it's her sanctuary, where the air tastes of hope and the world hums with quiet, blooming magic.

The wind blows high, the wind dips low,
it swirls above the frozen snow,
where prairies rest and softly dream,
wrapped in winter's silken seam.

Beneath the frost, so deep, so still,
a tender seedling stirs at will,
cradled in the earth's embrace,
in winter's quiet, sacred space.

Safe beneath the snow's soft kiss,
it dreams of warmth, of sun, of bliss,
of skies that sing, so clear, so wide—
the gentle touch of spring's warm tide.

For even in the coldest night,
a flicker stirs, a spark, a light,
a promise wrapped in winter's glow,
that life will rise, that life will grow.

Within the dark, the earth does hum,
a lullaby to what will come,
and when the thaw begins to sing,
the seed will bloom, and spread its wings.

It's raining again—
softly kissing the windowpane,
like an old friend returning,
bringing comfort with every drop.

I sigh and smile,
tea cradled in my hands,
as the rhythm of the rain sings to my soul.
I relish in this simple movement—
the earth drinking deeply,
flowers, trees, and leaves unfolding,
nourished by the sky's embrace.

And in time,
just as the rain feeds the soil,
it waters my heart,
awakening the parts of me that have been parched.

I know I'll stumble again one day—
trip over roots or lose my balance
on life's winding path.
But this time,
it won't shatter me like before.
I've grown stronger,
roots digging deeper into the earth,
anchoring me through the storm.
I've gathered sunlight in jars,
stored warmth for colder days,
and learned to bend like the willow
instead of breaking.

Now, when I fall,
it won't feel like a landslide,
won't bruise me down to the soul.
It'll be just a scrape—
a fleeting sting,
a reminder that I've built resilience
in the cracks where I once broke.

I have my safe harbors now—
places, people, and gentle words
to lean into when I need comfort.
I've gathered these treasures,
soft places to land
when life trips me up.

And I know,
when I fall,
I'll rise again—
dusted off,
a little wiser,
a little tougher,
and still reaching for the sky.

It's okay if today feels heavy,
if your heart drapes itself
like a rain-soaked coat
over your weary shoulders.
It's okay if your soul feels bland,
gray as a fog-covered morning,
or so sad it spills over
like rivers breaching their banks.

Let the feelings come—
give them room to stretch and breathe,
like wildflowers pushing through cracks
in the quiet, forgotten earth.
Feel how you inhale the air,
how your chest rises
like the sun peeking over hills
after a long, restless night.

It's okay to go slow,
to let the world blur a little
while you find your rhythm again.
Wrap yourself in the stillness,
like a soft cocoon,
and know that resting is not failing.

Some days, you're the seed,
buried deep, gathering strength.
Other days, you're the bloom,
reaching for the light.
But both are part of your becoming—
both are vital, both are worthy.

Tomorrow will come,
and with it, new light.
For now, let today be

just as it is—
a quiet, tender breath
in the vast garden of your life.

No one is mad at you.
No storm is brewing,
no shadow creeping closer.

No one is coming to take what is yours,
to silence you,
to punish your laughter,
to shrink you into silence.

No one calls you weak for weeping—
your tears are rain,
softening the soil,
making room for roots to deepen.

No one says you don't matter—
that voice is only an echo,
a whisper from the past,
a wind that no longer holds weight.

Breathe.
You are safe now.
Uncurl yourself from survival,
lift your face to the sun.
You can let go.
You can bloom.

Look down into the pond.
What do you see?
Beyond the koi weaving golden ribbons,
beyond the lotus, open and unafraid,
beyond the dragonflies skimming the surface—
look closer.

There—
who do you see?
Your own reflection, rippling softly,
a face that has weathered storms,
eyes that have held too much sorrow.

Take a deep breath.
Forgive yourself—
for carrying the weight too long,
for enduring what you never should have,
for believing survival meant silence.

It's okay. You are safe.
And deep in your heart,
you already know—
how to guard your peace,
how to bloom despite the murky past.

So don't lose yourself now.
Stay here. Stay present.
Watch the frogs leap with ease,
the lotus float, untouched by the water's depths,
the koi glide, steady and certain.

Now, look at yourself again.
You are strong.
You have always been strong.

My sister led me to the garden,
and for that, I'll always be grateful.
With dirt beneath my nails,
I've learned the language of growth—
patience in every sprout,
peace in every bloom.

The garden whispers,
slow down, breathe,
find joy in the smallest petals,
the tiniest seeds,
the warmth of the sun on your skin.

But more than that,
it has rooted us together,
side by side in the soil,
tending to something bigger than ourselves,
cultivating love—
one vegetable at a time.

*this poem was written to my little sister. I am so lucky to have you.
Thank you for you <3*

I feel low,
but not at my lowest—
like the sun veiled behind soft gray,
casting long shadows on my leaves.

But even in dim light,
I still stand,
still breathe,
still reach.

And that's enough.

It's okay to bend with the wind,
to rest in the quiet of the shade.
This moment is only passing through,
not here to stay.

So don't fear the clouds—
the sun is never truly gone.
It will break through,
warm your petals,
and you will rise again.

I am a tree;
I will not waver.
My roots sink deep,
woven into the earth's embrace,
steady, unshaken.

No storm can rip me from my ground,
no hands can tear me like a weed.
I do not beg to belong—
I already do.

I stand tall,
branches open to the sky,
leaves whispering their own truth.
I am strong,
fierce,
unbreakable.

And for the first time,
I grow for myself.

*this poem was inspired by something my therapist told me.*

I want to reach out,
to gather you in my arms,
an embrace that stretches through seasons,
through storms and sunrises,
back to where it all began.

I see you—
small, weary, weathered by the winds,
still standing, still reaching for the light.
I want to wrap you in warmth,
like the earth cradles its roots,
and whisper softly—

You are loved.
You are seen.
You are enough.

You always have been.

Autumn days are for watching—
the auburn leaves, like dancers, twirl,
their graceful descent a hymn to earth,
singing of cycles old as time.

They spiral down on whispered breeze,
soft and slow, as if to say,
*"Let go, dear heart, and trust the fall—
the soil will catch you, soft and kind."*

With every leaf that kisses ground,
a quiet wisdom stirs around—
for even trees, in their vast strength,
find grace in letting go,
releasing what they no longer need,
to grow in stillness,
and find their roots anew.

Like barley in a storm-tossed field,
you may bow low,
flattened by the weight of wind and rain,
your golden stems trembling,
bending to the earth's embrace.

But do not fear—
the storm cannot claim you.
Roots grip deep, anchored in ancient soil,
and though the tempest roars,
it cannot break what grows with purpose.

When the skies clear and the sun returns,
you rise, unyielding—
each blade kissed by light,
dew glistening like small triumphs,
the quiet proof of your strength.

In time, the storm becomes a memory,
the barley sways once more,
dancing freely with the breeze,
its rhythm a song of healing,
a hymn to endurance.

Sometimes,
it's worth standing still in the rain—
feeling each droplet kiss your skin,
tracing paths of silver down your cheeks,
soaking through the fabric of who you are.

Breathe.
Feel the rise and fall of your chest,
the steady rhythm of life within you.
You're alive,
you've weathered the storm,
you're strong.

And none of this—*none of it*—
was your fault.

Let the rain fall freely,
washing away the weight of old wounds,
softening the soil of your soul.
With every drop, let go.
Feel the earth beneath you,
clean, renewed.

And when the clouds part,
choose happiness.
Step into the sun,
a brighter version of you,
Ready to bloom.

How can you twist the wind to your will,
bending truth like branches in a storm?
You tear down what you built,
letting anger spread like wildfire,
just to stand among the ruins and say,
*"See? I was right."*

But storms don't last forever.
Eventually, even the fiercest gales die down,
leaving nothing but silence,
nothing but you.

And I—
I will not stand in the wreckage.
I will plant myself elsewhere,
where the soil is rich,
where the sun is warm,
where love grows instead of withers.

Good luck with your rage.
It will be a lonely harvest.

Dear little one,
love should be the warmth of the sun,
not the burn of its fire.
Love should be the gentle river,
not the tide that pulls you under.

Love should not make your heart shatter like glass,
nor teach you to walk on it, barefoot and bleeding.
Love should not make you flinch in fear,
nor shrink yourself to fit inside someone else's world.

No, little one—
that is not love. That is control.

Beyond this storm, there is a place
where love is soft as wildflower petals,
where kindness takes root like ivy,
where you do not have to beg to be seen.

A loving heart will never hurt you.
Love should not hurt.

Self-care wears many faces,
but one of the gentlest is this:
a warm cup of tea cradled in my hands,
steam curling like soft whispers,
as I sit outside on a sunlit summer's day.

The stool beneath me feels steady,
the air hums with life—
birdsong weaves through the trees,
a melody of belonging.
The breeze carries the scent of blooming wildflowers,
and the world feels quiet, whole.

I close my eyes, breathe deeply,
letting the warmth of the tea
melt into my chest,
and the rhythm of the earth remind me—
I am here.
I am enough.
I belong.

Of stardust and starlight,
we are born, and we shall die,
but my hope is this—
that my time of earth will forever lie,
bound to you, in moments shared,
in every breath and every prayer.

And when in time,
inevitably, we turn to dust,
to stardust and starlight, as all things must,
I too, hope that in the vast sky,
we will linger together, you and I.

In the endless dark, where all things fade,
I hope our love is a light that stays.

In the quiet of the morning, with you,
your tiny fingers, soft as dew,
grace the curve of my cheek,
and warmth blooms in my chest, so deep.

No words are needed, none at all—
in this silence, we are whole.
This simple touch, this fleeting grace,
says everything, in the sacred space.

I already know, without a sound,
that this moment is all I've ever wanted.
This, right here, is everything.

Feelings shift,
like the turning of the seasons,
chilled and heavy, they linger now,
but even storms have their reasons.

The weight of sorrow may cloud the skies,
but in time, the sun will rise,
breaking through the grey, the blue—
a quiet promise, ever true.

For just as seasons change their hue,
so too, will my heart find its view.

The sun will rise and shine once more,
casting light upon your weary shore.

Its warmth will kiss your tender face,
a gentle touch, a sweet embrace.

And when the night falls soft and deep,
the moon will rise, and stars will sweep,
like diamonds scattered in the sky,
to light your dreams as they pass by.

In every dawn, in every night,
the universe will hold you tight.

As long as I keep trying,
though I stumble, though I fall,
each bruise, a lesson carved in time,
I rise again, I stand tall.

With every step, though the road is long,
I walk, I press, my spirit strong.

I know that, one day, I will arrive—
and now, I believe I'm finally alive.

This journey, this fight,
is enough to make me whole,
for with each breath, I head my soul.

Let the leaves of your past drift gently to the ground,
crimson, gold, and brittle with time,
they no longer serve you,
their weight only holds you back.

Let them rest,
returning to the earth that once nourished them,
breaking down,
becoming rich soil for what's yet to grow.

And in time—
with sunlight on your face
and rain softening the edges of yesterday—
new leaves will unfurl,
tender and green,
adorning your branches,
proof that you are alive,
ever-changing, ever-healing.

Time and time again,
you say "yes" when your bones scream "no."
You push through, wear the mask,
smile as if the weight isn't crushing you.
But even the strongest masks crack,
and when yours finally shattered,
a little girl stepped out of the forest—
barefoot, trembling, lost.

Take her in.
Let her rest beneath the shade of your love.
Show her that honesty is not weakness,
that softness is still strength,
that even the strongest trees sway in the wind.

Remind her—
there is courage in tears,
healing in the quiet days,
when all she can do is watch the birds stitch the sky with
their wings.

Hold her.
Tell her she matters.
That even though her name feels like an echo,
she will find it again—
and this time, it will be hers to keep.

Don't shrink yourself,
don't press your feelings into tiny corners,
folding them small enough to fit in someone else's comfort.

Your emotions are not weeds—
they are wildflowers, untamed and real,
meant to bloom in the open air,
not hidden beneath the weight of expectation.

Speak your truth.
Let it rise like ivy climbing toward the sun,
let it be thorny if it must—
not everything beautiful is meant to be soft.

Liberation comes in full bloom,
not in careful pruning to please the world.

So, don't whisper what they want to hear.
Say what your soul has been aching to release.
Feel it. Own it. Let it grow.

I don't think I can forgive him
for the way he set fire to my garden,
watched the petals curl into ash,
and never once looked back.

But I've learned—
forgiveness isn't the only way forward.
I don't need to erase the scars,
or pretend the flames never touched me.

I just need to plant again,
to sink my hands into the earth,
to let the rain wash away what's dead
and make space for what's still alive.

I carry no forgiveness—only roots,
twisting toward the sun.

Wild horses vanish,
hoofbeats swallowed by the wind,
echoing in hollow hearts,
leaving sorrow in their wake.

Their beauty lingers,
a ghost beneath the setting sun,
a bittersweet memory,
fading like mist at dawn.

Yet hope still stirs,
carried in the hush of tall grass,
in the whisper of the wild,
a promise waiting to be found.

And there—amid the bluebonnets,
where earth and sky embrace,
two souls meet,
two hearts steady, beating as one.

I know this is hard,
I can feel the weight on your shoulders,
but the earth knows something we often forget:
a river doesn't apologize for its course,
a mountain doesn't explain its strength.
In the quiet of the forest,
trees stand tall,
unyielding,
their roots deep in the soil,
and they do not bend to every passing breeze.

Just like them,
you have the power to stand firm.
To say,
"No."
It's not a harsh word,
it's a shield,
a leaf that protects the tender stem,
a stream carving its own path.

And sometimes,
the most healing thing you can do
is let your boundaries grow,
nurture them with self-respect,
and trust that the world will still bloom around you.

So remember this,
Like the quiet whisper of the wind:
"No" is a complete sentence.
It is enough.

I feel like a pawn in his game,
a leaf tossed in the wind,
weightless, unnoticed,
twirling in the storm,
a thing to be discarded, forgotten.
His silence speaks louder than words,
and I am nothing in his eyes—
not his daughter,
not his kin,
just a shadow, fading into the cold.

But even the hardest winter
cannot stop the roots from growing.
Though the frost may bruise,
the earth remembers how to heal.
I am no longer that forgotten leaf,
I am the seed breaking through the soil,
pushing toward the sun,
claiming the space that is mine.

No more will I bend
to the winds of neglect,
no more will I shrink in silence,
I walk my path with the strength of mountains,
the wisdom of rivers that know how to carve their way,
I will bloom with the courage of a wildflower,
unapologetic, strong,
rooted in my truth.

I say no more,
and this time,
the earth echoes my resolve.

For years,
I believed your words,
like a seed trusting the soil,
hoping for warmth and growth.

But they only brought me thorns,
sharp, twisting through the heart,
a garden left untended,
with nothing but shadows.

I've learned now,
that words are like the wind—
shifting, uncertain,
promises drifting away like dandelion seeds,
only to be scattered in the storm.

But actions,
they are the rivers that carve their path,
the roots that hold steady through drought.

Your words no longer sway me,
for I've watched the patterns grow—
the same dry earth,
the same withered branches,
a tree that never blossoms.

You've shown me how little you care,
how little I matter in your world.

And so, I will step into the sunlight,
like a flower turning toward the sky,
no longer waiting for your words to rain down,
but trusting in the seasons that shape me.

I will protect myself,

and though your voice may still echo,
I will trust the roots that have grown deep,
the actions that speak louder than any breeze.

I save myself from you,
and as the leaves fall,
I make room for new growth,
one that is mine alone.

You have the right to step away,
like a tree shedding leaves in autumn—
releasing what no longer serves you.

Do not feel shame
for guarding your roots,
for planting yourself in richer soil,
for letting go of the thorns
that once drew blood.

You get to choose
how much of your sunlight
you give to those who cast shadows.
A passing breeze,
a distant echo,
or silence as vast as the sky—
the choice is yours.

Own it.
Wear it like wildflowers
growing freely in an open field.
You are finally tending to yourself,
and that is a kindness
the earth has always meant for you.

My heartbeat races—
quicker than the wind before a storm,
never quite at ease.

I walk with the weight of shadows,
always glancing over my shoulder,
reading the shifting air,
feeling the seasons turn like warning signs.

The storm is always near—
lurking in the cracks of silence,
waiting to strike at the drop of a hat.

But I am learning—
that not every gust becomes a hurricane,
not every shadow means danger.
The earth still breathes beneath my feet,
steady, unwavering.

And so, I inhale—
let the wind move through me,
without carrying me away.

I know how you feel,
I know the weight of the wind,
how it shakes you,
how it pulls at your edges,
like a lone leaf caught in a storm.

But listen—
you are not just a leaf,
you are the tree too.
Your roots run deep,
your soul was planted with purpose.

Find your anchor,
your steady rock amidst the tide.
Hold on—not just to life,
but to yourself.

You are worthy,
not despite your flaws,
but because of them.
You are the sun-kissed earth after rain,
the wildflower that refuses to bow.

So stand tall,
wrap your arms around yourself,
and breathe.
You've got this.

You learned to walk on eggshells,
each step a fragile dance,
as if the ground beneath you
might crack open with the weight of your fear.
Every move was careful,
every breath measured—
a dance on knives,
sharp and unforgiving.

You kept watch,
eyes wide like a sparrow in the storm,
tiny, trembling, but vigilant.
A little soldier,
standing guard at the gates of chaos,
making sure he didn't shift
like the seasons do—
sudden, with the snap of a finger.

You bore that weight,
a shield for your mother,
a wall for your little sister.
But even the strongest trees
can't grow under constant shadow.

Now, step out into the light.
Feel the soft earth beneath your feet,
free of shards and splinters.
Let the wind carry the heaviness away,
and let the sun touch your face.
The world can heal,
and so can you.

*"Be strong,"* they said.
So you built walls of silence,
telling yourself he couldn't hurt you.
You buried the ache,
bottled it in the hollow of your chest,
filling the quiet with emptiness.
You thought that's what strength meant—
to endure without breaking.

But, dear little one,
you were only a child.
No sapling should be asked to bear the weight
of a storm so fierce.

You deserved the gentle rain,
the soft light of dawn,
not the shadows that pressed so heavy.
Now, let the earth hold you.
Lay down that burden at last.
Feel the wind brush against your skin,
tender and alive,
whispering: *"You are safe now."*

And like the wildflowers after a frost,
you can bloom again.
Soft, radiant,
unburdened by the strength you were never meant to carry.

They should have watered your garden,
gentle hands tending the soil,
nurturing your roots with love and care,
so you could stretch toward the sun
and bloom in your time.

Instead, they left you parched,
dry earth cracking beneath your feet,
and you—
a tender sprout—
were forced to carry the rain for them,
giving what little you had,
when it was you who needed the light.

But gardens can heal,
even after neglect.
The rain will find you now,
the sun will warm your leaves,
and you will bloom—vivid, wild, unstoppable—
for yourself.

Do I wish things were different?
Maybe.
But I know this:
everything I've been through has shaped me,
like the rivers carve the stone,
like the wind sculpts the trees.

Though it has been hard,
I want to tell you something important, little one.
We are okay.
In spite of everything—
the storms, the shadows, the nights that stretched too
long—
we are still here.

Even the darkest hours cannot dim the light we carry
through this forest.
It flickers like fireflies in the night,
a quiet glow guiding us forward,
even when the path is unclear.

When the pain feels too much,
when we thought of giving it all away,
remember this:
the earth still cradles our roots.
The sun still rises,
and so do we.

We might bend,
swaying like the willow in the wind,
but we will never break.
Our strength is in our softness,
our resilience in our reaching.
We are still here.
And we are strong.

It's okay to cry,
to let the rain fall freely from your eyes,
to let the storm gather in your chest,
dark clouds swirling,
thunder rumbling beneath your skin.

It's okay to yell,
to release the winds that have been held back too long,
to let them howl through the trees of your soul,
clearing the air,
unleashing the roar that you've kept buried.

It's okay to feel the full force of the storm.
Let it brew, let it rage,
for storms are but a part of the earth's rhythm,
and so are your emotions.

Stay in the feelings.
Stand firm like an oak in the tempest,
let the wind shake your branches,
but know this:
*You are rooted.*
*You are strong.*

Though you weren't allowed to show your storms,
know that they are as natural as rain.
They do not define you,
but they do heal you.

Let them stay—
for they will pass.
Like the storm that clears the sky,
your heart will find the calm,
and the sun will return,
warmer and brighter than before.

Did you know that kale can grow even in winter?
that even when the frost settles deep,
biting at its leaves,
it still stands, still thrives—unshaken.

Have you ever noticed how scarlet kale,
draped in snow,
becomes even more beautiful?
The cold does not break it;
it deepens its color,
turning it a richer, bolder shade of purple.

And maybe, dear one,
you are like that kale—
enduring the frost,
weathering the storms,
only to emerge more vibrant,
more brilliant than before.

The cold does not define you,
but it shapes you,
and through it all,
you are still growing.

Treat your mind with care,
soft hands, gentle words—
it is a garden, after all,
one that flourishes with love.

It needs sunlight in the form of warmth,
rainfall in the form of rest,
and soil rich with self-compassion.

So water it with kindness,
pull the weeds of self-doubt,
and plant seeds of patience.

Tend to yourself as you would a fragile bloom,
and watch—
slowly, steadily—
how you begin to grow.

Weed out the thoughts that strangle your roots—
the ones that whisper doubt,
that tangle around your mind like ivy,
choking out the light.

Yes, I know they've been there for years,
their roots deep, their grip firm.
But they do not serve you.
So pull them out, one by one.

It may take weeks, months, even seasons—
but with each weed removed,
you make room for something new.

And one day, when your mind is clear,
when the soil is rich and open,
you will finally have space
to plant the hydrangeas you've always loved,
to watch them bloom in shades of blue and violet,
soft and full—like the peace you have found.

When your roots outgrow their space,
do not be afraid to move.
You are not meant to stay confined,
bound by soil that no longer nourishes you.

Repot yourself in something bigger,
something that gives you room to stretch,
to heal, to flourish.

And don't forget the drainage—
let go of what no longer serves you,
so your roots can drink in love,
without drowning in the past.

You are meant to grow,
to thrive,
to bloom.

You're like a spirited squirrel—
leaping from branch to branch,
a burst of wild, unbridled energy
that fills the forest with laughter.

Your joy is infectious,
like sunbeams breaking through stormy clouds,
lifting my heart, brightening even my darkest days.

You are the warm glow after rain,
my hope amid the tempest,
a constant reminder that even chaos can be beautiful.

When anxiety dims my sky,
your presence is the gentle breeze
that clears away the gloom,
calming my restless mind.

If I can be your safe harbor,
your own remedy for turbulent moments,
then you are the healing light that steadies my soul.

Together, we dance in nature's embrace—
finding solace, strength, and love in every bound.

*this poem was inspired by Jung Hoseok (of BTS) by a moment of his concert 'Hope on the Stage Tour'.*

Your scent drifts like a whisper of sunshine,
soft, radiant, wrapped in warmth.
Oh, to be held by you—
to let your golden embrace mend my frayed edges,
to quiet the restless storms within.

You remind me that healing is gentle,
that even in the harshest soil,
bright petals will unfurl,
reaching for the light,
believing in brighter tomorrows.

Your hues—sun-drenched yellow, ember-kissed orange—
glow like hope in the garden of my soul.
Oh, Calendula,
a flower, a balm, a promise—
that things will be okay.

I don't want to burden anyone—
with my feelings,
with my pain.
But I know now,
that's the child in me whispering,
afraid of being too much,
afraid of being seen,
afraid of the sting of rejection.

These feelings press against my ribs,
tight like the walls of a seed,
holding me in place,
telling me to shrink, to stay small.
But I am learning—
learning to push through the dark,
like a sprout cracking open,
reaching for the sun,
even when the earth feels heavy above me.

Some days, fear lingers,
a shadow from the past,
telling me to stay quiet, to stay safe.
Even in my thirties,
I still brace for the echo of voices
that once told me I was too much.

But I am not too much.
I am becoming.
And like the wind bends the branches
but never breaks the tree,
I will not break.

I will speak my pain,
I will speak my truth,
and I will let my words bloom.

I wish I could forget
the way your words cut—
how you said I remind you of her,
your failure.

I wish I could erase
the tight knot in my chest,
the way your smile twisted
as you let the words fall,
sharp as shears against my stem.

You pruned me off,
not to nurture, not to save—
but to discard,
to watch me wither
against the cold concrete,
petals scattered like drops of blood.

But seasons change,
and I am not done blooming.
What you left behind,
the earth has reclaimed—
roots deepening, branches stretching.

Spring is here,
and I will rise again.

I am the scapegoat,
the black sheep wandering alone—
but solitude has become my second skin,
stitched together with quiet resilience.

I have learned to cherish those who stay,
like roots that refuse to wither,
even when the cold sets in.
Yet, the shadows of abandonment still linger,
whispering doubts like wind through hollow trees.

I hold on too tightly,
clinging like ivy desperate for something to climb,
afraid that if I let go,
I will fall into the emptiness I have always known.

But I am learning.
Learning that love is not a vine to strangle,
but a garden to nurture—
that true connection will not wilt when given space to
breathe.

I will work on it.
I will grow.
I will trust that I am enough, even when I stand alone.

I used to bend like a willow in the wind,
bending over backwards for others,
leaving my roots unwatered,
my leaves drooping,
thirsting for my own care.

But time has taught me
the wisdom of seasons,
the quiet strength of the oak,
how it grows, slowly but steadily,
by nourishing its own roots.

Now, I am learning to say no,
like a flower that closes at dusk,
protecting its energy,
refusing to bloom when the world asks too much.

I am reclaiming my space,
putting myself first,
and it feels as natural as the sunrise—
there is no shame in the quiet healing
that comes from rest,
from saying no to what drains me,
and yes to what nurtures me.

This is the path of self-love,
and it's as necessary as rain to the soil.
It's healthy.
It's growth.

Sometimes, I wonder why you stood still,
silent in the storm's rage,
watching the chaos unfold
without a word, without a fight.

But I know, in the quiet of our hearts,
you were the shelter beneath the oak tree,
taking the brunt of the storm,
your branches bending,
your roots holding firm.

Behind closed doors,
you weathered the worst of it,
shielding us like the wind shields the forest,
carrying the weight of a thousand unseen battles.
For that, I am forever grateful—
though I wish the winds had never blown so fierce.

But now, together,
we will heal like the meadow after the rain,
soft and steady,
nourished by the promise of new blooms,
lifting each other up,
soaring like birds in the endless sky,
free to feel the warmth of the sun,
and the peace of the open field.

*this poem was written for my mom. She is the strongest person I know.*

Sometimes, I wonder if this feeling
will always nestle in my heart,
quiet and persistent,
like a cloud that lingers too long in the sky.
Part of me thinks it just might,
but that's okay—
for my past is like the roots of an ancient tree,
deep and tangled,
woven into the soil of who I've become.
Though those roots were once bruised and broken,
they've stretched and healed,
pushing toward the light.
I have grown from the wounds,
like flowers unfurling after the storm.

I am thriving,
no longer chasing the horizon,
for the journey itself is enough.
I no longer seek the finishing line,
for healing is not a destination—
it is the river flowing,
the seasons changing,
and the earth turning,
never rushing, always becoming.

And as I work on myself,
like a gardener tending her soil,
I will plant seeds of self-discovery,
watering them with patience.
In the process, I'll meet myself
with compassion,
with each new bloom
bringing me closer
to the quiet peace
of the forest at dawn.

I've hidden my pain like a thorn-covered vine,
carefully draped in a facade of leaves,
my smile a delicate flower bloomed from the cracks,
bought by the weight of quiet suffering.
I've spoken lightly of my hurt,
like a breeze whispering through the branches,
but beneath it, the roots of my truth run deep.

People tell me I'm lying,
but there's nothing to gain from this shadow I cast.
I've made life harder,
by pretending the storm inside me is just a light rain,
my emotions hiding beneath a veil
that only stifles the wind of my soul.

Can't you see how the silence chokes me?
That's why I'm trying to speak louder now,
to shed this "good girl" mask,
like leaves falling in autumn,
unafraid of the winter winds that follow.
I'm peeling back the layers,
rooting for the first time in the soil of my own voice,
no longer afraid of what others might say,
or fearing that I'll be cast out like fallen petals.

Now, as I grow into my own light,
I find the courage to stand tall,
like a tree that finally reaches for the sun,
unfurling its branches wide,
no longer bound to the earth by the weight
of others' expectations.

I won't pass this on,
this fear that once held me in the shadows,
to the next generation of seeds.

I'll teach them how to grow with honesty,
and let their roots run free,
nourished by the soil of self-love.

Feelings rush in like a restless wind,
whispering doubts, stirring storms—
but winds always change,
they pass, they fade, they shift.

Do not let the current sweep you away.
Root yourself like an ancient tree,
dig deep into the earth of your own strength.
Let the storm howl—
you will not break.

This moment is a passing season,
and you,
you are the mountain it cannot move.

No matter how many feet
trample over you,
how many voices whisper
that you are nothing,
a bother, a burden—
do not believe them.

They do not see your strength.

Like the dandelion,
growing wild in cracked pavement,
brushed aside, stepped on, ignored—
you will rise again.

The wind will carry your seeds
to places they never imagined,
and you will bloom,
bright and golden,
proving that even the smallest flower
can thrive against all odds.

Some days will feel heavier than others,
like the weight of the sky pressing down,
like your petals are curling inward,
fading, fragile—
a rose caught in the cold.

But fret not, little one,
this is not the end.

Even the softest bloom must shed its petals,
must rest before it flourishes again.
Beneath the surface, life is stirring.
A new bud will rise,
unfurling in its own time,
reaching for the sun,
ready to bloom once more.

Inside my greenhouse, time slows.
The air is warm, laced with the scent of earth,
soft chatter of leaves swaying in the breeze.
Birdsong drifts through the glass,
a melody of morning, of renewal.

My hands sink into the soil,
rich, cool, alive between my fingers.
With every seed pressed into the earth,
with every sprout stretching toward the light,
I feel it, too—
the quiet magic of growing,
of healing,
of becoming.

Do you remember, as a child,
kneeling in fields of green,
fingers sifting through clover,
searching, hoping—
two leaves, three, never four?

And then—
that breathless moment,
when luck unfolded in your hands,
a tiny treasure, a whispered miracle?

Don't forget that wonder,
that spark of joy untouched by time.
It still lives in you,
waiting to be found again.

Thirteen and alone,
adrift in a storm, roots exposed,
no shelter, no hands to pull me back.

You were the wave that shattered my world,
left me gasping in the wreckage.
I cried for help,
but the wind carried my voice away.

A flower, whitering,
petals torn by hands that should have protected,
innocence dragged through the dirt.

Still, I reached—
toward you, toward love, toward something soft.
I shouldn't have had to beg for sunlight,
shouldn't have had to mend what was never mine to break.

But even the most fragile flowers
find a way to bloom again.

*this poem was inspired by the song 'The Pilot </3' from ONE OK ROCK.*

Next time you wish to brighten someone's day,
why not gift them something that lingers,
something that grows?

Not just a bouquet—beautiful, fleeting—
but a plant or a seed packet, small and full of promise,
a living thing that thrives with gentle hands,
a quiet reminder of care, of patience, of time.

Let them watch new leaves unfurl,
let them tend to its roots,
let them see for themselves—
that with love, even the smallest seed can flourish.

Go for a walk.
Pause. Listen.
Let the world whisper to you.

Hear the birds weave melodies through the trees,
feel the sun press warmth against your skin,
breathe in the crisp scent of rain-kissed moss,
let the earth cradle your every step.

In this moment—
you are *here*,
you are *whole*,
you are *alive*.

They say the night is darkest before dawn.
So sit awhile—
on the edge of the shore,
or by your open window,
let the salty waves kiss your toes,
let the cool air brush against your skin.

Gaze toward the horizon.
Even now, the sky is shifting,
a whisper of gold at the edges of night.
Hold on. Breathe.

Soon—
the sun will rise,
painting the world in light once more.

Stretch out your hand—
toward the purple butterfly bush.
Wait.
A monarch hovers, sipping nectar,
its wings trembling like whispered breath.

Then—softly—it lands on your finger,
delicate, weightless, alive.
Hold still. Watch closely.
See the sun catch the gold in its wings,
the quiet rhythm of its fluttering heart.

Two weeks—that's all it has.
And yet, it soars,
dancing through the air as if eternity is held
in each fragile beat.

Perhaps, like the butterfly,
we, too, should live
as if every moment is a masterpiece.

Sometimes, we rush—
too lost in the noise of our days
to notice the quiet miracles around us.

The dewdrop-laced spiderweb,
woven like silver threads in the grass.
A bird, tilting its head,
singing a song only the wind understands.
The frog, still as a stone,
watching ripples dance upon the lake.
An ant, tireless in its purpose,
building a world beneath our feet.
The squirrel, leaping from branch to branch,
cradling an acorn like a precious gem.

So, stop.
Listen.
Let the world reveal itself to you.
In the smallest details,
life whispers its most beautiful secrets.

The tree never shrinks itself,
never wonders if it takes up too much space.
It simply stretches skyward,
reaching for the sun without apology.

It does not count its branches,
nor question their direction—
it lets them unfurl, wild and free,
dancing with the wind.

Its roots sink deep into the earth,
steady, unwavering,
a silent reminder—
to ground ourselves,
to stand tall,
to grow without fear.

You are the sunlight warming my face,
gently drying the tears I thought would never end,
a golden whisper reminding me—
*I am not alone.*

You are my friend.
Though miles may stretch between us,
your presence is as certain as dawn,
as steady as the tides.

I am not joking when I say
you are warmth itself—
a quiet light, freely given,
spilling joy, hope, and laughter
like morning rays through parted blinds.

You lift me, even when I shrink into shadows.
Even when I say, *I am too much,*
you remind me—
*I am enough.*
I am not a burden.
I am not a bother.

And you—
you are my sunlight,
my soft golden proof
that today will be a good day.

The little girl had dreams too big for her tiny hands,
too vast for the walls that tried to hold them in.
So she dreamed—
of kingdoms woven from stardust,
of dragons with shimmering scales,
of secret doorways hidden in the roots of ancient trees.

The night sky cradled her whispers,
the moon a patient guardian,
the stars—her silent companions.
She would send her wishes into the cosmos,
hoping the wind might carry them someplace real.

Endless hours she spent beneath the constellations,
tracing her future in the patterns of the night.
Would she make it?
Would she ever reach the other side?

She did.

And now, every evening,
she thanks the stars and the moon,
for listening when no one else would,
for keeping her dreams alive,
for reminding her that magic
had always lived inside her.

Let the fog wrap around you,
soft as a whispered lullaby.
Breathe it in—slow, deep, steady.
Feel its cool touch on your skin,
a quiet promise that you are held.

Let it settle,
let it soothe,
let it remind you—
even in the mist,
everything will be alright.

I am trying to find space in my heart
to let you back in—
but this time, on my terms, not yours.
Because you don't deserve me,
but I might still need you.
Maybe that makes me selfish,
but no matter how hard I try,
I can't seem to uproot you from my soul.
If only I could, I would—
tear you out like stubborn weeds
that refuse to let the garden breathe.

So here I am, brick by brick,
building walls to protect what's left—
only letting you glimpse
a tiny sprout of me,
not the whole wild garden I used to be.
Because I still can't trust you
with the tender shoots of my heart,
the petals you once crushed
without a second thought.

I know you don't deserve a third chance,
but how do I prune you out completely
without losing parts of myself?
I stand at the edge of my own wilderness,
wondering if cutting you out
means cutting down memories
that once bloomed in spring.

But I'll learn—
to plant new seeds,
to tend to the wounds,
and to let the wildflowers grow
with or without you.

Sun,
bathe me in your golden embrace,
like the sunflower stretching skyward,
face lifted, heart open.

Fill me with light,
let me stand strong,
rooted in hope,
growing toward tomorrow.

From just the tone and pitch of your voice,
I can sense the shifting weather of your mood—
storm clouds gathering, or sunshine breaking through.
That's what living with you taught me:
to read the sky of someone's soul
by the way their words hang in the air.
And now you act surprised
when I know how you feel
just from the way you say "hello" on the phone?
You created this; you created me—
a heart that hears before words are spoken,
a soul that feels the tremor of another's hurt.

It's because of you
that I'm attuned to the world's quiet ache,
that I want to ease the burdens of others,
because I know how heavy they can be.
It's because of you
that I'm gentle with the bruised
and careful with the broken.

This is the gift you gave me—
one I've learned to cherish,
a quality I'm proud to carry.
But now I know:
I must water my own roots first,
tend to my own garden,
before helping others bloom.

Thank you.
For making me sensitive,
for showing me the power of compassion—
but also for teaching me,
in your own roundabout way,
that it's okay to put myself first.

No matter how much you long to escape,
your roots remain, winding deep beneath the soil.

You cannot cut them away—
to sever them is to wither,
to lose the strength that holds you upright.

Instead, let them be.
Let them rest beneath the earth,
a quiet foundation, unseen but steady,
nourishing every bloom you become.

Love and learn,
plant your roots deep in the soil,
get your hands dirty in the earth,
let the rain wash away the dust,
and rise again.

Healing is wild,
a tangled vine,
a flower blooming from cracked stone—
unraveling is part of becoming.

Broken is beautiful,
like a tree scarred by the storm,
yet it stands stronger,
after it learns to bend,
after it learns to grow.

*this poem was inspired by the song 'The Pilot </3' from ONE OK ROCK.

I know how much you've carried,
the weight of unspoken words,
the quiet sacrifices,
the love you pour into everyone else,
as if you were the soil,
nourishing the world around you.

But listen—
even the earth needs rain,
even the sun rests behind the moon.
For all the love you so freely give,
for all the light you scatter like seeds,
let some of it bloom within you.

You deserve to be your own garden,
to be watered,
to be held by the warmth you give to others.

You deserve that love, too.

The wind runs its fingers through my hair,
carrying away the last of my worries.
My head feels lighter—
no longer tangled in the shadows of your judgment,
no longer bending beneath the weight of your gaze.

I don't wonder anymore
what you think of me.
Like autumn leaves surrendering to the breeze,
I have let go.

And I feel free.

You think we don't feel it,
the pull of your storm,
hot one minute, cold the next,
like wind tearing through a fragile bloom.

You take,
then leave us gasping for air,
only to return,
as if we're just the earth for your roots to latch onto,
no apology, just more of the same—
like a vine that chokes the life it claims to love.

But look at the damage,
look at the wildflower bent and bruised,
still standing, though scarred—
how much more of me do I need to lose
before I remember how to grow without you?

*this poem was inspired by the song 'NASTY' from ONE OK ROCK.*

Don't let him win.
He has taken enough—
left shadows where sunlight should be,
planted doubt where love should have grown.

But the storm is passing,
and now, it's time.
Time to fight for yourself,
to reclaim the soil he tried to poison.

And if the battle gets messy,
let it be—
even the earth must break open for seeds to grow.

Like the lotus,
I will rise,
unfold my petals,
bloom defiantly—
even in the mud, even in the pain.

*this poem was inspired by Min Yoongi (of BTS).*

I know what it's like
to hurt in silence—
to bury the pain
like roots deep underground,
twisting in the dark.

That's why I want to be the sunlight
breaking through the canopy,
to make sure no one else
wilts unseen in the shadows.
That's why I listen,
why I reach out with open hands—
to remind others
they are not alone
in the forest of their hurt.

That's why I speak of my own pain,
show my scars like wildflower petals—
fragile, yet vibrant—
because I never used to.
I know now
that sharing our stories
is like rain falling gently
on parched soil—
it helps us grow,
feel rooted,
seen, heard,
connected.

In the quiet of understanding,
we find comfort—
a garden where we are not alone
in our struggles,
but blooming together
through the storms.

I will be your shield—
a towering tree,
roots grounded deep,
branches stretched wide,
protecting you from the storm.

No more harm will touch you—
I'll be the shelter
when thunder crashes,
the soft moss underfoot
when the world feels sharp.

You are safe, little one,
nestled in the quiet of the forest,
where sunlight filters through leaves,
and the wind hums a lullaby.
Here, wrapped in nature's embrace,
I promise—
nothing bad will reach you.

A friend once whispered to me,
*"One foot in front of the other,"*
and it felt heavy—
but also like the light
at the end of a very dark tunnel.

*"Just walk slowly,"* she said,
like guiding me through a forest path,
and I did just that—
every day.
One foot in front of the other,
moving through tangled roots
and shadowed trails,
learning that the journey
isn't always swift or easy,
but it's still forward.

Slowly, I realized—
this is all I need to do
to navigate life—
just keep moving.
It's okay to go slow,
to let the moss grow beneath my feet,
as long as I am moving ahead.

And for her,
the friend who taught me
to walk through the dark
with quiet courage,
I'll forever be grateful.

She was my compass
when I lost my way—
my steady guide,
showing up every day

with comfort and hugs,
like a soft rain
nurturing the wildflowers of my heart.

I wish for everyone
to have a friend like that—
a soul who lights your path
when the forest feels too dense,
a gentle reminder
that even slow steps
are steps toward healing.

Sometimes,
progress feels like a whisper,
a seed buried deep in the soil—
quiet, unseen, almost too slow to notice.
But don't feel discouraged,
or abandon the journey now—

Because growth takes time,
roots stretch in silence,
reaching through the dark,
finding strength in the stillness.
Sure, progress may feel slow,
but slowly and surely,
you are growing—
and one day, you will bloom.

Every step counts,
like raindrops gathering in a stream,
like sunlight coaxing buds to unfurl.
Just keep going—
show up, even when giving up
seems easier.
You are weaving something beautiful
with every small, steady movement.

Trust in your roots,
trust in the unfolding.
You will get there,
petal by petal,
bloom by bloom.

Please—
make me a promise, right now.
Like the sun never hides from the sky,
like the river never silences its song,
promise me you won't swallow your pain.

It's not fair that you share your laughter
with the world,
but keep your tears locked away in the dark.

Please—
let someone in,
like the earth lets the rain fall
so it can bloom again.

Promise me,
when the weight feels too heavy,
you won't carry it alone.

Let your voice rise like the wind,
let your sorrow flow like a stream—
you were never meant to wither in silence.

I didn't want to die,
I wanted you to feel the weight
of the storm inside me,
the thorns of heartbreak
that tangled in my chest.

I wanted you to understand—
to see the deep roots of my pain,
how it grew from hurt,
how it wrapped around everything
we built and now,
slowly unraveled.

But I've learned—
I can't make you feel what I do.
I can only let my heart
replant itself,
breathe again like fresh earth after rain,
and grow stronger in the quiet healing.

It feels strange without you here,
like a tree missing its branches,
unbalanced, but still standing.
I've come to understand—
blood doesn't make you family,
love does,
and that was something we never shared.

So I'll carry this truth with me,
like a seed in the earth,
ready to bloom,
nurtured by my own hands,
rooted in the love I've built
for myself.

My mind was once a storm-torn field,
thick with thorns, heavy with shadows,
a place where nothing good could grow.

For years, I believed it was set in stone—
that the soil of my past was too ruined to heal.

But now, through gentle hands and patient tending,
through therapy and time,
I have learned how to *change the soil,*
to pull the weeds of old wounds,
to plant seeds where only sorrow once lived.

So please—don't wait as long as I did.
Don't let the past define you,
don't believe that pain is all you are.

Because you are not your scars.
You are the gardener of your own mind,
and with care, even the roughest ground
can bloom again.

Look how far you've come—
once, his words were a storm,
pulling you under,
waves crashing in your chest.

But now,
a message arrives,
and you stand like the shoreline,
calm, unwavering,
watching the tide roll in
without letting it sweep you away.

You think, you breathe,
you choose your words with steady hands,
rooted, firm,
holding your ground
without breaking the bridge.

You did good.
And you'll keep doing good.
And if the day comes
to draw the final line in the sand,
to let the tide carry him away,
I know you'll do that too.

I guess I wanted to save him—
pull him from the tide,
guide him to solid ground,
but some souls aren't searching for the shore.

You can't rescue someone
who doesn't reach for your hand.
You can't pour sunlight into a heart
that refuses to bloom.

And he will never understand your pain—
some minds are wired like stone,
some hearts are locked doors
with no key.

So let go.

Let the waves carry him where they may.
You were never meant to drown
just to keep someone else afloat.

Yes—
he is your father,
but love should not bruise,
should not leave scars,
should not feel like walking barefoot
on shattered glass.

You have spent years
shielding everyone else,
holding up the weight of storms
that were never yours to carry.
But now—
it's your time.

Let your boundaries bloom like wildflowers,
rooted deep, unshaken by the wind.
Wrap yourself in kindness,
like the gentle hush of leaves at dusk.
No space for thorns,
no room for shadows
that dim your light.

Protect yourself the way
you have protected everyone else.

I wish the winds had blown differently,
that the stars had aligned in another way—
I wish he could be the person I needed him to be,
but the earth does not bend to our wishes.

I want him, I do,
but not like this.
Not through the storms,
the broken promises like shattered glass,
not through the thorns that wound every time we touch.

So, I stand here—
with the weight of it all,
picking up the pieces,
letting the healing rain fall gently
to soften the jagged edges,
and slowly,
I piece myself together again.

I'll walk barefoot on the soft grass of self-love,
growing into something whole,
stronger than the cracks that once defined me.

Sometimes the hardest things to let go of
are the ones that hurt the most.
But forward, always forward—
I move through the garden of my own peace,
and I leave the past behind.

I do believe in second chances,
like the first bloom after winter's grasp—
soft petals pushing through frozen earth,
offering forgiveness to the cold.

But I've learned to listen,
not just to the songs of promises,
but to the rustle of leaves in the wind,
to the truth that actions whisper.

Once might be a mistake,
like a branch bending too far,
twice an accident,
a storm that passes with the dawn—
but the third time,
like a persistent drought,
is a pattern I cannot ignore.

I've planted seeds of trust,
and I know when to nurture them,
and when to let them go,
to let the soil rest,
and wait for new roots to grow.

Oh,
what I'd give to be a child again—
to run through the wild, green grass,
feet bare, kissing the earth,
laughing as the wind tugs at my hair.

I'd crawl on hands and knees,
the denim on my legs stained with life—
green from the soft blades,
a secret mark of nature's touch.

I'd search for four-leaf clovers,
tiny miracles hiding in the earth,
as my heart danced in rhythm with the breeze,
smiling—
unburdened by the weight of grown-up worries.

No thoughts of time,
no questions of why or how,
just the simple joy of being—
in the embrace of nature's arms,
where peace grows in every corner,
and each moment is enough.

Sometimes,
I dream of sprouting wings,
and soaring far beyond the horizon,
into the embrace of the soft, endless sky.

I rise,
carried by the gentle winds,
my wings cutting through the air—
a brief escape,
a moment of peace,
where the weight of the world
is nothing but a distant memory,
and the clouds beneath me
whisper the secrets of the universe.

But even as I rest there,
I know the earth calls me back,
with its roots and rhythms,
reminding me that life is waiting.
And though I long for solace,
I won't let the clouds keep me forever,
for I am made of strength and light—
I'll return,
and face the world again,
with wings renewed
and heart open to the journey.

Listen, kid,
your instincts are like the river—
steady, knowing, always flowing home.
They have carried you through storms,
through tangled roots and restless tides,
guiding you even when the path was unclear.

You just need to remember—
trust the pull of your own current,
let the wind of your knowing move you forward.
They have brought you this far,
and they will never lead you astray.

A tree does not stop reaching for the sky,
even when the wind steals a branch.
It does not mourn what was lost forever—
it grows around the wound,
weaving strength into its scars.

You, too, have weathered storms,
been broken, bent, torn apart—
yet here you are, still standing.
Like the tree, you are meant to heal.

So on the days when the weight feels unbearable,
when the past tugs at your roots,
remember:
Living means healing.
And healing means growing.

At times,
I feel left behind—
adrift like a lone leaf in the wind,
watching as others move forward,
their laughter echoing in the distance.

I have always been the black sheep,
the scapegoat,
cast in roles I never chose.
And though I know I am more than this,
the feeling lingers,
like winter's relentless frost,
freezing me in place.

I remind myself—
this is only a season,
a passing storm,
not the shape of forever.

I know you don't mean to leave me behind,
but still, the distance settles like snow,
quiet, heavy, unshaken.

Yet spring always comes.
These feelings will thaw,
the ice will melt,
and in time,
we will meet again beneath softer skies.

It's okay to lean on others
when the weight feels too much—
you don't have to journey alone,
like a lone leaf drifting
in a vast, empty sky.

I am here for you—
a rooted tree,
strong enough to shelter you,
when the winds of life grow harsh.
You don't have to carry it all—
I'll stand beside you,
a branch to hold you steady,
when the storms come.

Lean on me—
and together, we'll weather the seasons.
You are never alone.
I'm here for you, always—
in the sun, the rain,
and every step in between.

Rain falls soft,
like petals drifting on a breeze,
whispering through the leaves,
a quiet symphony of renewal.
I treasure these days—
when time slows to a soft pause,
sitting by the window,
a warm cup of tea cradled in my hands,
the steam rising, mingling with the mist.

I watch—
the rain's delicate dance,
fingers of water tracing paths down the glass,
as the world outside softens and sighs.
I listen—
to the rhythm of the earth being kissed,
each drop a tiny promise,
a balm for the soul,
healing in its stillness.

In this quiet,
I find a peace I can't put into words,
a balm for the weariness within.
The rain, like a gentle mother,
nurtures me,
as I breathe in the soothing whispers of the storm.

I'm not as happy as I play—
a painted smile to hide decay.
Like sunlight on a wilting vine,
I mask the parts that ache and pine.

Is this mask enough to deceive?
Can you glimpse the webs I weave?
Like ivy climbing crumbling walls,
I'm grasping at a sky that falls.

Beneath each grin, I scream for air—
a bird that beats its wings in snare.
Trapped in a cage of quiet lies,
my soul longs for unclouded skies.

I'm drowning more than I'm admitting—
like roots submerged but never quitting.
One day, I'll break the soil's tight hold—
and bloom where truth can still unfold.

Can you hear the echo of my call?
A voice lost where the shadows fall—
like wind that weeps through barren trees,
a whispered plea on weary knees.

I reach for light, yet fall below—
roots tangled where no blossoms grow.
Please don't leave me in this hollow,
where night devours each breath I follow.

Alone, adrift in darkened skies,
I search for hands, for hopeful ties—
a lighthouse through the storm's embrace,
a guiding star in endless space.

I need a guide to find my way,
to gather fragments where I lay—
a river seeking banks to fill,
a seed that longs to break the still.

Please, pull me from this silent sea—
help me return to what was me.
Let petals bloom from shattered stone,
and roots find earth to call their own.

Why does my mind betray me so?
Whispering shadows I cannot outgrow,
intrusive tides that swell and rise,
pulling me beneath stormy skies.
I am adrift in waves unseen,
a prisoner bound within my mind's keen.

I struggle, clawing at unseen chains,
yearning to break free from these pains—
free of the currents that twist and tear,
free from the tempest that swells in air.
Yet with every step, the maze expands,
like tangled roots in shifting sands.

Why do I turn against myself?
Why do I carve wounds upon this shelf,
feeding the ache, lost in its call,
falling like leaves in a silent fall?
Spirals I cannot break,
patterns woven by each mistake.

Who am I without this pain?
Can I bloom, after such rain?
And why must I endure alone—
like a tree in the forest, all unknown?

But deep within, beneath the strife,
there's a quiet seed of life.
Perhaps, with time, and gentle care,
I'll find the strength to heal the air.
Roots will stretch, and flowers bloom,
the storm within will fade to room.

To some,
he might have seemed like shelter—
a towering tree casting shade,
but in truth,
he was choking your roots,
blocking your light.

But no more.
It's time to step out of his shadow,
to let the sun kiss your leaves,
and feel the warmth you've always deserved.

Take it slow—
one step into the open,
one breath of fresh air,
one bloom at a time.
I know you can do it.
Grow toward the sky—
your light is waiting.

Don't fear the unknown—
don't shrink from change—
don't resist the call to evolve.
Be wary instead of standing still,
of letting roots grow stagnant in hardened soil.

The magic of blooming
happens at the edge of comfort,
where wildflowers dare to reach
toward the light,
even when the wind howls.

Keep pushing through the dirt,
keep breathing through the storm—
growth may feel uncertain,
but it's how petals unfurl
and dreams take root.

You can make it.
One brave breath at a time.

Like Zoe Skylar said:
*"For a star to be born,*
*one thing must happen—*
*a gaseous nebula*
*must collapse.*

*So collapse.*
*Crumble."*
Let yourself break open
like a seed splitting in the dark earth,
like a wave crashing to the shore.

*"This is not your destruction—*
*this is your birth."*
The universe rearranging itself
to make space for your light,
a brilliant blaze
rising from the ruins.

You are not falling apart—
you are forming
into something luminous,
into something vast,
into something new.

I'm learning to be here,
rooted like a steadfast oak,
leaning in to listen,
to feel the breeze of your words
and the river of your feelings
flow through me.

I'm learning to stay tuned—
like petals opening
to the sun's warmth,
I'm reaching for your light,
holding space for your storms.

Your feelings,
like wildflowers blooming
in unexpected places,
are precious to me—
vulnerable, real,
worthy of care.

I want to be your garden—
a safe place to grow,
a calm place to rest,
where your thoughts can wander
and find comfort.

Because your wellbeing
is the heartbeat of this place
we're building together—
and I am here,
rooted, present,
growing with you.

It's okay to cry,
let the tears fall like rain,
pouring from the sky,
clearing the path to peace.

You are not alone—
like the roots beneath the earth,
I am here,
a steady presence in your storm,
a gentle hand in the wind.

Cry, and let the earth
hold your sorrow.
You are safe,
in this moment,
in this space of healing.

I'm here for you,
as the river is to the sea,
as the sun is to the horizon,
always,
unwavering,
with open arms,
ready to cradle your heart.

Listen.
It's not your job to carry the weight of the world.
Like a tree, you don't have to shelter every storm.
It's my job to hold the rain for you,
to offer you the roots you can lean into,
and the branches that will cradle you through the winds.

I want the responsibility,
the privilege,
of tending to your spirit,
like the earth nurtures the seeds,
giving them space to grow—
with patience, with care,
until you bloom again.

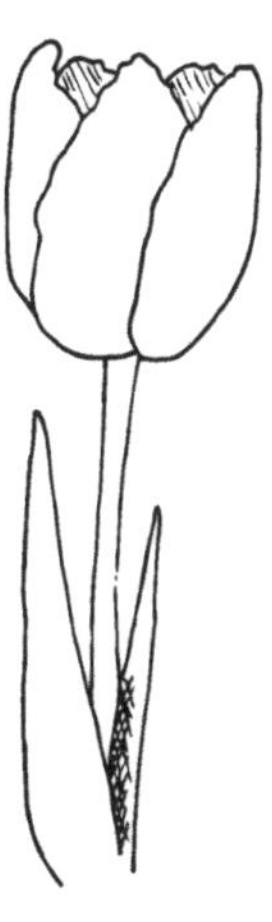

# the bloom

When your garden is alive with color, a masterpiece of petals and greenery, do not turn away from it. Do not let its beauty slip into the background, taken for granted. Even in full bloom, your garden needs you—your love, your hands tending to its roots, your quiet presence among the rustling leaves. The flowers that grace your world still crave nourishment, still need your gentle care to continue thriving. And when the frost begins its slow approach, they will need your preparation, your patience, your understanding.

So step into your garden—some days, not to work, not to fix, but simply to exist. To pause in the sun-dappled quiet and whisper to yourself, *"I did this. I built this. I poured love into this, and look how it thrives."* Let yourself marvel at what you've nurtured. You have worked tirelessly to reach this place. You have fought through storms, pulled weeds from the tangled depths, and coaxed life from the soil. *You have earned this moment—to rest, to breathe, to bask in the beauty of all you have grown.*

When you are in bloom, the world will take notice. Bees will hum in your presence, drawn to your sweetness, your light. Butterflies will dance around you, and others— kind souls, wandering hearts—will find themselves gravitating toward your warmth. Share your joy, let your radiance spill over, but always tend to yourself first. A garden that gives and gives without replenishing its own soil will soon wither. *Nurture your own roots, and only then can you truly give to others.*

Healing has no finish line, no grand moment of completion. Even in the height of bloom, there will still be weeds to pluck, soil to enrich, petals to tend. And sometimes, despite all your care, life will send

unexpected storms—rain when you least expect it, winds
that shake your branches. Do not fear these moments.
They are not ruin; they are renewal. If you must pause, if
you must retrace your steps and gather yourself, do so with-
out shame. *Healing is not a straight path but a winding one,
full of twists, turns, and new directions. Walk it as you need.*
        But oh, *look at how far you have come.*
Do you remember the days when darkness wrapped around
you like thick ivy, when hope felt distant, when you could
not see beyond the weight of your own mind? Look at
where you stand now. The birds are singing. The air is
fragrant with wildflowers and summer rain.

*You are here, and it is beautiful. You made it.*

And that, in itself, is extraordinary.

Sunshine kneels in the garden, her hands moving with gentle purpose as she weeds out the plants that choke and hinder growth. She whispers quiet apologies to the stubborn intruders, pulling them free and setting them aside, knowing it's all part of helping the garden thrive.

She sprinkles fertilizer like a blessing, enriching the soil with love and nutrients, making sure every plant has what it needs to reach its fullest potential. As she waters each one, she sits beside them, letting the cool splash of droplets kiss her arms. Sunshine watches the vines stretch and curl, inspecting each leaf with careful eyes, searching for spots or mildew that could signal distress.

Her fingers trace the stems of the tomatoes, cucumbers, and melons, her heart heavy but resolute. Pruning is necessary—she knows this. Without it, the plants would grow wild, spreading their energy too thin, chasing every direction instead of flourishing in one. With a pair of small, silver shears, she trims the extra growth, murmuring words of comfort.

"I know," she sighs softly, snipping away the wayward tendrils. "It's hard to let go, but it's how you'll thrive." Sunshine can't help but feel a pang of sadness as she prunes—the way the bright green leaves fall to the soil, their purpose fulfilled. But she also knows that this careful tending, this delicate balance of cutting back and nurturing, is part of caretaking. It's love with boundaries, allowing the plants to put their energy where it matters most, so they can fruit and blossom with all their might.

As she sits back, she breathes in the earthy scent of the garden, feeling the bittersweetness melt into something softer—like letting go of old habits to make space for new dreams. Nature knows the art of balance, and as the sun warms her back, Sunshine knows she's doing what's best for her leafy companions. Sometimes, healing means trimming away the excess, making room for life to bloom.

You didn't deserve what happened—
the storm that tore through your branches,
the weight that bent your stem.
But you deserve to heal,
to feel sunlight on your leaves again.

Healing doesn't erase the past,
it plants new roots where the ground once cracked—
soft shoots sprouting from old scars,
wildflowers reclaiming a field
once burned by pain.

You are not broken—
you are becoming.
You are blooming,
like a stubborn blossom
pushing through the ashes,
and that's where your power begins—
in the courage to rise,
to unfurl,
to grow toward the light.

Care for what blooms before you,
love it, nurture it—
let it unfurl beneath your touch,
soft and steady, like spring rain.

Hold its warmth in your heart,
carry it forward like seeds on the wind,
never forgetting the roots that shaped you,
but knowing the past is only soil—
a place to grow from, not to dwell.

Step gently, step bravely,
one foot in front of the other,
breathing in the present,
where light filters through the trees,
where new blossoms rise to meet you.

I long to cradle my heart with tender hands,
to treat myself as I would a garden of blooms,
where each petal is kissed by the sun,
and the roots are nourished by gentle rains.

The stranger within, harsh and unkind,
yearns for the soft touch I give the earth—
a whisper of leaves in the breeze,
a moment of stillness in the growing woods.

I wish to speak to myself as I do the stars,
with words of warmth that heal the cold,
to believe in the kindness that stirs in me,
as rivers carve their paths through stone.

Can I learn to love, as the forest loves the dawn,
to trust the quiet strength within,
and bloom, as flowers do in the first light,
unfolding into who I'm meant to be?

*"Would it be wrong to speak my truth?"*
The voice inside my head would whisper,
like the winds tugging at the branches,
and once, I'd bend like the willow—
the answer was always *"yes,"*
but today, the answer is rooted firmly: *"No."*

It's never wrong to let the storm inside me speak—
whether the clouds are heavy or the sun is shining,
whether my heart is wild with joy, or quiet with sorrow.
For I've learned to listen to my own voice,
and like a tree learning to stretch toward the sun,
I grow stronger with each word I say.

There was a time I'd feel guilty,
like a fragile petal afraid to fall,
but now, I know—
self-care is not selfish,
it's a garden where I nurture myself to bloom.
I plant my needs with pride,
water them with compassion,
and let them take root in the soil of my soul.

And though the world may sway like the wind,
I stand tall,
knowing that the earth is mine to tend,
and I am fucking proud of what I've grown.

I am the girl who loves too much,
who pours herself like rain over dry earth,
who stretches like ivy, reaching for warmth.

But I'd rather be the girl who loves too much
than the one who withholds like an unyielding drought,
than the one whose heart is a barren field, untouched by
spring.

Let me spill over,
let me bloom wild,
let me love—even if it aches—
for love is not a weakness,
but the root of all things that grow.

You are one of a kind,
a rare bloom in a field of green.
A *purple tulip*—soft yet strong,
standing tall beneath the weight of the sky.

Even in the dark,
your elegance glows,
petals whispering stories of quiet resilience.

Even in sorrow,
you do not wither.
I admire you—
for your strength,
for your endurance,
for the way you rise toward the light,
even when the night lingers long.

You are so much stronger than you know.

Have you ever wandered through the forest,
found yourself standing before
the tallest, oldest tree—
its roots thick as ancient secrets,
its branches stretching wide
like open arms?

That's the mother tree.
She knows the forest by heart,
recognizes her kin,
whispers to the saplings swaying below.
She draws water from the deep earth,
guiding it up through her veins,
then releases it, drop by drop,
to nourish the shallow-rooted seedlings,
teaching them how to grow strong.

She shares her wisdom
through the underground web,
sounding alarms when storms approach,
making space for her children—
pulling back her own roots
to give them room to thrive.
She doesn't just stand tall;
she nurtures, protects, and sustains.

And like the mother tree,
we too must share our stories,
nurture those who come after us—
pass down self-love like a legacy,
carve space for future hearts to bloom.
We are rooted in the past,
but our branches reach forward,
sheltering those who follow,
guiding them toward the sun.

My head feels lighter,
like spring air after a long winter—
and for the first time in forever,
my mind feels like a safe space—
a kind space, too.

Speaking harshly to myself
feels strange now,
like trying to plant thorns
in soil made soft with rain.
The bitter words sit heavy on my tongue,
no longer belonging—
like weeds in a garden
that's finally learned to thrive.

There's no room for cruelty anymore,
only room for the soft bloom
of wildflowers—
sunlit petals stretching
toward a gentler sky,
roots weaving through my thoughts,
grounding me in kindness.

I've made a home for myself here—
a garden where tenderness grows,
and I nurture it daily,
letting love take root
in the place where thorns once thrived.

I've never been fond of "change"—
it feels like an untamed river,
rushing forward, never asking if I'm ready.

But evolving? That, I can embrace.
Like trees shedding their leaves,
not in loss, but in quiet preparation
for something new.

Walking in two directions at once
is impossible—
a seed cannot stay buried
and bloom at the same time.
So here I stand,
on the trembling edge of transformation,
heart pounding like rain before a storm,
anxious, uncertain—
but alive.
t
I inhale the fear,
exhale resistance.
Because I know—
with change comes growth,
and with growth,
I will bloom into something
wild and beautiful,
rooted and free.

The roses are beautiful,
but beauty can bite.
Their thorns, sharp as whispered warnings,
cut deep if you get too close.

They've learned to guard themselves,
petals soft, but defenses high—
a habit born from survival.

Yet beneath the thorns,
there is more than armor,
more than war.

There is fragrance,
there is bloom,
there is resilience dressed in red.

We are not just what wounds—
we are what grows,
what heals,
what loves despite it all.

Don't you dare come running back,
trampling through my garden,
crushing the petals I've nursed to bloom,
uprooting the peace I've sown with care.

I have tilled this soil with my own hands,
pulled the weeds,
let the rain cleanse me,
let the sun mend the cracks you left behind.

You don't get to come crawling back,
unraveling what I have nurtured,
what I have fought to grow.

No.
This garden is mine now.
And I will not let you ruin it again.

You said you loved me,
but love does not crush tender petals
or stomp through gardens meant to bloom.

Time and time again,
your words were sunlight,
but your actions were storms,
ripping roots, breaking stems,
leaving me to wither.

And later, when the vines of time
should have softened your heart,
you told me I did not matter—
that your vendetta was worth more
than your own daughter.

But I am not the wilted flower you left behind.
I have learned to grow in spite of you,
to bloom where you swore I'd never rise.

And now—
my garden is mine,
untouched by your footsteps,
thriving without your shade.

Protect your garden,
protect your peace.
Not everyone who enters
comes with gentle hands.

You've spent seasons
nurturing the roots,
coaxing blooms from the soil
with love and patience.
Don't let careless footsteps
crush what you've grown.

If someone stunts your growth,
drains your light,
wilts your spirit—
pull them out like a weed,
without apology.

Your garden is sacred.
Let only the kind-hearted stay,
the ones who water you
instead of taking your rain.

I wandered too long in the shadows,
carrying the weight of endless nights,
so much so, I feared
the sun might never find me again.

But now—
light filters through the leaves,
casting gold upon my skin.
Colors I once forgot come rushing back,
petals unfurl, reaching for the sky.

My garden hums with life,
each bloom a promise,
each breeze a whisper—
stay, breathe, live.

And now I know—
there is too much beauty in this world
to ever let the darkness keep me.

My knees ache
from carrying the weight of storms—
stones of anxiety, guilt, and sorrow
pressing heavy on my chest.

I thought I was alone,
wilting in the shadows.
But then—
a hand reached out,
then another, and another.
Friends.
Not just passing voices,
but roots intertwining,
holding me steady in the wind.

I still fear I'm too much,
that my pain will wear them down,
that my stories will turn to weeds.
But they stay.
Sometimes, they don't speak at all—
just listen,
just hold me.
And that's enough.

To the friends who became my sun,
who watered my weary soul—
thank you.
Because of you,
I am learning to bloom.

*this poem was written to all the friends I've made along the way <3*

Don't shrink from your scars—
they are roots of resilience,
branches that weathered the storm.
Stand tall, unshaken,
let the sunlight kiss your wounds.

Wear your pain like petals,
soft but strong,
proof that you've blossomed despite the frost.

And when you bloom,
don't be afraid to share your flowers.
A single bloom,
offered with kindness,
can take root in someone else's garden,
filling empty spaces with color,
with hope.

Maybe they, too,
have been waiting for a sign
that spring will come again.

You are beautiful—
no matter the stories you've whispered to your reflection,
no matter the shadows that tried to dim your light.

You are beautiful.
Inside and out,
like the first bloom of spring,
like petals kissed by the sun.

You shimmer,
you glow,
even when you don't see it.

Don't let the world steal your radiance.
You are a calendula—
bright, resilient, healing.
A flower that thrives,
even after the storm.

Don't listen to your fears—
they are nothing but creeping vines,
twisting, tangling, trying to choke your light.

They steal your growth,
like weeds that do not belong,
feeding on doubt,
draining your soil of strength.

But you—
you are meant to flourish.
Let your roots stretch wide,
deep and untamed,
so full of life
that fear has nowhere left to take hold.

Let the weeds wither,
let the noise fade,
and bloom,
wild and free.

Before I rise,
like a phoenix, crowned in crimson flame,
or a blossom breaking winter's icy claim,
I must learn the art of surrender—
to twirl amidst the embers' glow,
to waltz with every golden leaf
as it tumbles into fire's embrace,
a fragile farewell to what once was.

Only then,
from the ash of withered dreams
and the frost of long-lost seasons,
can I bloom anew.

If anything,
autumn is a quiet hymn,
a golden whisper that all things fade—
leaves fall, skies dim,
and even the strongest branches
bow to time's steady hand.

But within the decay,
a promise stirs:
the earth will soften,
the frost will melt,
and you will bloom again.

A friend beside you in the garden is gold—
together, hands in the soil,
you sift through the tangled roots of bad thoughts,
plucking them gently, one by one,
as sunlight warms the earth beneath your palms.

You tend the flowers already blooming—
petals trembling with quiet hope—
watering them with the gentle rain
of laughter, love, and whispered dreams.

And with every drop of care,
you see life stirring—yours and theirs—
a shared bloom opening wide,
steps growing lighter as burdens fall like withered leaves.

In unity, the weight of the world softens;
together, you unearth hidden seeds of joy,
buried deep under the soil of yesterday.
Here, your mind unfurls its greenest leaves,
stretching skyward through rich, healing earth.

The garden grows as you grow—
carefree, vibrant,
alive.

Each day,
pause, and look within.
Breathe deeply—
do you feel it?
The scent of flowers unfurling,
petals soft and radiant,
colors vibrant with life.

They bloom, thriving,
rooted in the quiet care you've given,
watered by your perseverance,
nourished by your light.
You did that.

Let those words settle,
like sunlight on your skin.
Read them again—slowly—
and feel the warmth spreading,
golden and alive,
through every vein,
a quiet reminder:
the garden within you is flourishing.

In your hands,
a freshly cut bouquet of flowers,
petals soft as whispers,
fragrant as a summer breeze,
each bloom alive with vibrant hues.

Instead of giving them away,
pause.
Feel their weight, their delicate beauty.
Gift them to yourself—
not as an indulgence,
but as a reminder:

You are loved.
You are enough.
Just as these flowers bloom for the sun,
you bloom for the light within you.
Cherish this moment,
this gift of tenderness,
and let it heal the parts of you
that has forgotten how to feel whole.

Every rose wears its thorns—
a shield against hands that take too much,
a whisper of lessons learned in the wind.

It's okay to protect yourself,
to grow defenses where the wounds once were,
but don't let fear keep you from the sun.

Not every hand will pluck,
not every touch will wound.
There are gentle ones too—
soft as rain, steady as roots.

Love will find you,
like light reaching through the branches,
like a garden tended with care.
When the time is right,
let yourself bloom.

I look up at the vast, endless sky,
midnight stretched like velvet,
stitched with silver constellations.

The full moon hums above me,
casting its quiet glow,
a soft reminder that even in darkness,
there is light.

I breathe in the cold night air,
crisp against my skin,
cleansing, stilling the echoes of the past.

No thoughts, no weight—
just the hush of the universe,
whispering that I have made it through,
that I am here,
and I am free.

Do you know what it feels like to lose someone?
I do—
but this is different.

You are still here,
yet slipping through my fingers
like autumn leaves caught in the wind.

I am scared.
You were meant to be my shelter,
my steady ground—
but you turned into the storm,
the lion with teeth bared,
the wildfire that burned my trust to ash.

Tears glisten beneath the full moon's glow,
its quiet light cradling my sorrow.
I know I'm losing you,
and though your roots once ran deep in my heart,
I must be the one to walk away.

Some things are meant to be let go—
to make space for something new to bloom.

I wholeheartedly agree
with what Kim Namjoon said:
*"True revenge is to be strong. To survive. To protect."*

Not in the way fire devours,
or thorns pierce—
but in the way trees stand tall
after every storm,
their roots sinking deeper,
their leaves still reaching for the sun.

To live well,
don't let anger take root like weeds,
don't let revenge poison the soil of your soul.

Instead, grow.
Bloom in kindness,
radiate light,
thrive despite it all.

Because that, my friend,
is the most beautiful revenge of all.

There were days you felt like a three-headed dragon,
breathing fire, smoke curling from your lips,
your roar echoing in the hollow of my ribs.
Did my pain fuel you?
Did you feast on my fear?

I learned to lock my stories away,
sealing them tight like a chest buried beneath the earth,
because every word I gave you
became a weapon in your hands.

But now,
I have outgrown the shadows of your flames.
I have walked through the ashes and found life again.
Most people are not like you—
they do not strike with sharpened tongues,
they do not turn love into war.

I do not have to shrink,
do not have to measure each word like a fragile glass bead.
I will not flinch at kindness.
I will not live in fear.

And those who carry fire in their hands,
ready to burn—
I will not stand close enough to be caught in the blaze.

Your needs, your desires—
they are not second place,
not shadows beneath someone else's sun.
You are the roots, the seed, the bloom.

Blood is not the thread that binds—
love is.
Not obligation, but trust.
Not duty, but respect.
A garden does not flourish
because it is planted in the same soil,
but because it is nurtured,
watered,
cherished.

You will find your own meadow,
your own wild, radiant family,
where love is given freely,
where you can finally bloom.

Please others less,
and nourish your own roots more.
Like a tree standing tall in the wild,
let your strength come from within,
not from the hands that reach for your branches.

Learn to bloom for yourself,
not for the eyes that only admire.
Feel the sun on your skin,
without waiting for permission to stand in its light.

Let your "no" be as natural as the tide retreating,
as effortless as leaves drifting on the wind.
Boundaries are not walls—
they are the rivers that guide you home.

Grow freely. Breathe deeply.
You are enough.

Hot or cold,
Good or bad—
my childhood was a storm
of shifting winds and unyielding skies.
But she—
my mother—
gathered us like fragile seeds,
carrying us away each weekend
to the shelter of family and friends
whose roots ran deep,
whose love felt like sunlight after rain.

In her way, she was our shield,
a sturdy oak in a world of gusts,
bending but never breaking.
She whispered us safe,
guarding us from the storm's fury,
quietly speaking him down,
easing the thunder that rumbled within him.
For that, I am grateful—
but I see now the weight she carried.

And now, she is like a wildflower
breaking free of the frost,
stepping into the warmth of her own spring,
rediscovering the bloom that was buried
beneath the shadow of his storm.
Her petals stretch wide,
and the fierce beauty she once hid
rises with the sun, unafraid.

*this poem was written for my mom. She is the strongest person I know.*

Shimmer, shimmer,
make the world around us glimmer.
If only you could see through my eyes,
you'd sparkle like the starlit skies.
A dance of light, a trail of gold.
In every moment, a story untold.
If you could only feel the glow,
you'd become the magic that you show.

You are kind.
You are loving.
You are so much more than the words you were told
when you were small,
when he tried to dim your light.

But now—
stand tall,
like the sunflower in your garden,
face the sun,
and remember your worth.
Even when the world tried to convince you
that you had none.

Be gentle with yourself.
Let the soft wind kiss your skin,
and the birds dance around your head,
their songs a reminder of your freedom.
Watch the sun rise and fall,
its warmth touching you,
like a hand on your heart,
whispering: *"You are enough."*

Don't forget yourself.
You are rooted in the earth,
strong as the oak,
with branches that reach for the sky—
wild, untamed,
just as you were always meant to be.

You are loved,
like sunlight warming the quiet earth.
you are valued,
like rain quenching a parched field.
You've done so much good—
planted seeds in others' gardens,
nurtured blossoms not your own.

But now, dear soul,
it's time to turn to your own garden.
Feel the soil beneath your hands,
rich and ready for new beginnings.
Pull the weeds of worry,
let the gentle rain of self-care fall.
With time,
your blooms will unfurl,
vibrant, wild, and wholly yours.

It's okay to cry,
to let the rain pour from your soul,
watering the parts of you
that have long been left thirsty.

Climb to the mountaintop,
let the wind carry your voice,
a scream, a whisper, a release—
everything you were told to bury,
everything you once hid behind closed doors.

Your feelings are real,
wild as the ocean,
deep as the roots of an ancient tree.
No one can take them from you,
they are yours—
and they are meant to bloom.

Sometimes, I lay on my kids' trampoline,
back pressed against the woven threads of childhood,
eyes tracing the slow dance of clouds,
the effortless glide of birds,
the silver streak of a plane cutting through the blue.

And I wonder—
what would it be like to fly?
To drift on the wind, untethered,
to roam without the weight of doubt,
without the fear of not belonging,
without the voice that whispers, *you are not enough.*

Then, a bird tilts its wings,
catching the light just right,
and I realize—
I *am* that bird.

I can take flight,
from garden to garden,
from dream to dream,
unbound,
unapologetic,
free.

Hoofbeats thunder,
rhythms drumming against the earth,
wind tangles in my hair,
a whisper of freedom, wild and untamed.

No thoughts—just breath,
air crisp against my skin,
lungs filled with the scent of open fields,
ff sun-warmed grass and endless sky.

Bareback, we race,
through golden meadows, into the trees,
where shadows dance and secrets linger.
Toward the quiet, toward the light,
toward a place where nothing weighs me down.

Just me and my horse,
bound by trust, by rhythm,
by the unspoken language of wild things.
No burdens. No chains.
Only the gallop of my heart,
and the call of the open world.

You've carried the weight of the world,
like roots gripping tight to soil,
holding everything together,
but in the process,
you've lost yourself—
a leaf swept away in the storm.

It's time to let go,
to release the branches you've clung to,
for there's no need to lose yourself completely
just to keep holding on to someone
who lets you fade like the last light of dusk.

Remember, the seasons change,
and so must you—
you are not a vine that must always twist to others' will.
You are a wildflower,
meant to bloom where you are,
to stand tall in your own sun,
unafraid to reach for the sky.

You learn to guard yourself
like a sapling in the storm,
branches trembling but unwavering,
and now—
use that shield to protect your garden,
your sacred space where peace blooms,
where joy unfurls like petals in the sun.

Nurture what you've planted—
the seeds of your laughter,
the flowers of your spirit,
the roots of your resilience.
Protect it from the thorns he casts,
from the shadows that try to choke your light.

Because he thrives on your wilting,
on seeing the rain fall when the sun should shine.
His happiness is a storm cloud,
but you, you are the sunrise
that breaks through the dark.

Don't give him that power—
don't let him steal your joy.
Let your garden grow strong,
wild and untamed,
where only love and kindness are allowed to take root.
Let the breeze of your peace
whisper through every leaf,
reminding you that your heart is your own—
and nothing can take that away.

This ends with me,
like a river carving its own path,
I refuse to let the storms of the past
flow into my children's hearts.
I won't watch them drown
in the same bitter waters I once did.
I say no more.
This ends here, on my watch.

I will not raise my voice like a thunderstorm,
turning their world into a place of fear,
I won't stifle their laughter,
I won't silence their joy
like a wilting flower afraid to bloom.
I won't tell them to dim their light,
to watch the shadows,
to cower in the corners of the world.
No more.

I will teach them that they are the sun,
shining bright,
not a flicker in the dark.
I will be their shield—
a tree standing tall,
roots deep in love and protection.
I will tell them they matter,
that they are as worthy as the earth itself,
and that the world, though full of storms,
is also a garden—
full of good, gentle souls,
and that the thorns are just part of the journey.

I will teach them to walk around the shadows,
to stand tall,
to walk with kindness,

and never forget their worth,
for they are made of stardust and dreams.
This will be my gift to them—
a garden of strength,
where love blooms wild,
and their roots are firm in the ground of truth.

Relax—
Breathe—
Feel the air fill your lungs,
the wind that whispers through the trees,
carrying away the weight of years.
You are free.
Free as the river flowing,
unstopped by rocks,
moving forward, steady and sure.

You've been free for years,
though the shadow of his grasp still lingers,
a fleeting cloud passing across your sky.
But you don't need to look over your shoulder anymore,
the earth beneath you solid,
the ground firm beneath your feet.

No longer do you have to bend like a willow,
always bowing to satisfy his whims.
You don't have to tread lightly on the path,
worried about every step,
worried about the storm that could rise with a word.

You've found your sanctuary,
a place where the flowers bloom,
and your voice carries on the wind,
unhindered, strong, and true.

You are safe.
You are home,
where the birds sing without fear
and the sky stretches wide,
inviting you to breathe in the beauty of your freedom.

And in this moment—

you are free.
A wildflower in a field,
rooted in your own truth,
unfurling to the sun,
embracing the peace you've earned.

As a child,
I wandered through forests of silence,
branches whispering secrets I couldn't share.
I stood apart,
a lone tree in an empty field,
watching others bloom together,
but never quite knowing how to reach them.

Music became my river,
words my shelter from the storm.
They called me "the weird one,"
but I learned to walk alone,
feet pressing softly against the earth,
each step a quiet song of survival.

Now, the path is different.
I am no longer alone.
I've found hands that hold steady in the wind,
voices that echo my laughter,
souls that understand without needing words.

Side by side, we walk beneath open skies,
roots entwined, yet free.
We share the sunlight,
the rain,
the seasons of joy and sorrow.

And that is enough—
more than enough—
to build a world where we all belong.

Listen—
you are not the sun meant to warm their world,
nor the rain to quench their thirst.
You are not the soil where their unfulfilled dreams
should take root and grow.

I know you long to see them smile,
but some storms are not yours to calm,
some hunger not yours to feed.
You were not born to carry their weight,
to be the branches they climb
when their own ground feels unsteady.

No—
let them weather their own seasons.
Let them face their own skies.
You are the wildflower breaking through the cracks,
the river forging its own course,
the wind untangling itself from the past.

This life is yours—
grow, bloom, be free.

As long as I can remember,
I chased perfection like the sun,
always just out of reach.
I climbed higher, ran faster,
pushed past exhaustion,
hoping you'd see me bloom.

But you looked past me,
eyes tracing the sky,
naming the stars after other children,
never noticing the garden
wilting at your feet.

I burned myself into light,
hoping to shine bright enough—
but the flames only left me ash.
Still, I rose,
again and again,
smiling through the embers,
only to be unseen once more.

But seasons change.
Now, I water myself.
No longer waiting for your sun,
I let the rain heal me,
let the wind carry away the weight
of all I was never meant to hold.
And still—
I grow.

I have always valued my quiet,
wrapped myself in the safety of silence,
the "good girl" who never spoke too loud,
never let the world see the storms within.

But I am tired of being the echo,
swallowed by empty rooms.
I want to share my story,
to let my voice rise like birds at dawn,
because somewhere, someone is listening—
someone who needs to know
they are not alone.

Pain, when spoken, does not break us.
It binds us, bridges the space between souls,
turns isolation into light.
So I will step forward,
even when my hands shake,
even when my voice wavers.

I will walk toward the open world,
toward those I have yet to meet,
soulmates waiting like stars in the sky—
I only need to look up.

Love was a language I never learned,
its meaning tangled in raised voices,
in doors slammed and silence stretched too thin.
I thought love meant disappearing,
shrinking, avoiding the fire
so I wouldn't get burned.

But then, there was you.

I spoke, and you listened—
not just to my words,
but to the unspoken weight in my chest,
the echoes of a past lined with ash and embers.
You stayed, steady as the earth beneath my feet,
took my hand and said,
*"Let's walk together."*

And so, we did.

Love is not just magic;
it is tending, nurturing, growing.
It is the gentle pruning of fears,
the daily watering of trust,
the patient bloom of understanding.
We do not leave it to fate—
we work for it,
as one tends a garden,
with open hands and open hearts,
and in return, it flourishes.

Ours is not the love of fleeting flames,
but of deep roots and soft petals,
of stardust and soil,
of something real, something lasting.
And for that, I am grateful.

*this poem was written for my husband <3*

I was a cup cracked and leaking,
spilling over with doubt,
while you were the steady stream,
filling the spaces I thought were lost.

You showed me kindness—
not just in your touch,
but in the way the sun filters through the trees,
in the way the waves kiss the shore,
in the way the earth holds steady beneath my feet.

You taught me love—
not the kind that wavers,
but the kind that lingers like wildflowers in bloom,
soft, unwavering, alive.

You taught me that healing
is in the warmth of a simple hug,
in the whisper of wind through the leaves,
in the quiet knowing that I am enough.

And for the first time,
I am not just half of anything—
I am whole.

*this poem was written for my husband <3

Please, don't be afraid to love.
Don't fear the open sky,
the breeze that brushes against your petals,
the rain that falls, uninvited but kind.

Don't be afraid to help and give,
because somewhere, the right people wait—
the ones who will see you.
Not just your smile,
but the love tucked within your pain,
like wildflowers growing in the cracks of stone.

The right people will gently kneel beside you,
hands in the soil of your garden,
helping you water it with patience,
tending to your roots until they feel strong again.
Together, you will watch it bloom,
petals unfurling in the sunlight,
colors you thought you'd forgotten.

Don't be afraid to let them in,
like the morning light slipping through the trees,
soft and warm.
Don't be afraid to let them love you
for the beauty of being wholly, deeply you.

Their love is not what you need
to make your garden bloom.
Should they have given it to you?
Yes.
But they didn't.

And now, you are no longer a child.
You are the gardener of your own soul,
tending the soil with your hands,
nourishing the roots with your own heart.

You don't need their love—
you need *yours.*
Your love is the sunlight,
the rain that falls soft and steady,
the warmth that the seeds crave,
and the patience that helps them grow.

Love yourself,
little one,
the way the earth loves the first bloom,
gentle, unhurried,
but constant.

And watch your garden bloom—
wild and free,
colors you've never known,
a beauty that only you could cultivate.

You have done a lot,
more than you know,
and through it all, you kept growing,
even when the world seemed to crumble.

You did not deserve what happened,
but in the quiet of your soul,
you took all that dust,
and let it settle,
like ashes turning to fertile soil.

From that earth, you grew—
a wildflower, reaching toward the sun,
your petals unfolding with grace,
and though the winds were fierce,
you stood strong,
turning the pain into gold,
bright as the first rays of dawn.

I love you.
I love you for every scar,
for every tear that watered your roots,
for every step that led you through the storm.

You are doing good,
more than you can see,
and you are enough—
like the oak that grows from a single seed,
strong, steady, and true.

You gave your all,
poured your light into empty hands,
but even then, it wasn't enough for him.

Still, the sun does not dim itself
for those who refuse to feel its warmth.
The river does not stop flowing
because one refuses to drink.

You do not need his love
to know your own worth.
You are the roots that hold steady,
the wildflower that blooms without permission,
the mountain that stands, unshaken.

You are perfect on your own—
whole as the sky, vast as the ocean,
a universe unto yourself.

Beautiful, aren't they?
The petals you once thought would never unfurl,
now stretching toward the sun,
soft, radiant, alive.

But don't forget—growth doesn't end here.
Keep watering, keep tending,
remind yourself, again and again,
that you are worthy of this bloom.

Gently brush the dust from your petals,
run your fingers along the edges of your own beauty,
and whisper,
*"I'm proud of you."*

And in return, your garden will sigh in gratitude,
blossoming even brighter,
a living testament to all the love you've given yourself.

I am kind,
soft as petals kissed by morning dew,
but do not mistake my gentleness for fragility.
The storm I survived carved rivers in my soul,
yet I chose to bloom instead of break.

There is fire beneath this quiet surface,
a pulse of thunder in my veins.
A beast sleeps within me,
its breath steady, its roar waiting.

I am the calm before the storm,
the roots that refuse to be unearthed.
Strength is not always loud—
sometimes, it is the patience to rise again,
unyielding, unstoppable.

I keep searching for answers,
flipping through the pages of us,
but no matter how many times I reread,
the story still bleeds.

The good times were petals in the breeze,
soft, fleeting, a whisper of warmth—
but the bad ones took root,
weighing me down like tangled vines,
pulling me deeper into the dark.

There is no fairytale ending
when the scars run this deep.
So, I must let go,
shed this chapter like autumn leaves,
step into the sun,
and learn to bloom without you.

Be gentle, like the morning sun
spilling warmth over frozen ground.
You don't know what storms have left someone barren,
what roots have withered beneath their skin.

Please—scatter kindness like wildflower seeds,
let it take root in unseen places.
A single drop of kindness can soften
even the driest earth,
a single word can lift a spirit
like rain coaxing buds into bloom.

Make someone smile,
like the first breeze of spring after a long winter.
Bring light where there was only shadow.
Give them what you never had—
and in doing so,
watch your own heart flourish.

Because healing is not just taking,
but also giving,
watering the world with love,
until one day,
you, too, are surrounded by a garden
that grew from your kindness.

Sand shifts between my toes,
waves whisper secrets to the shore.
The salty breeze runs its fingers through my hair,
tracing the lines of my skin,
as I sink into the earth's quiet embrace.

The sun hums warmth into my bones,
and in the distance—
a song, light as the wind.

I turn, eyes tracing the sky,
where a flash of color flutters,
weightless, untamed—
a hummingbird,
hovering, defying gravity,
wings a blur against the endless blue.

What is it doing here,
so far from the flowers,
from the safety of green canopies?

And yet—
it soars, it lingers,
it moves even against the wind,
as if to say,
you, too, can find your place anywhere,
even where you least expect to bloom.

Sometimes, you must prune your thoughts,
like trimming a tomato vine,
like shaping the branches of a fruit tree,
guiding growth toward the light.

Some memories cling like overgrown stems,
draining your energy,
stealing the sunlight meant for new blooms.

So cut them back.
Let them fall like withered leaves,
returning to the earth,
making space for something new.

Feel yourself grow lighter,
stronger,
free to blossom where joy can reach you.

Little one—
let me make you a promise:
we will meet where the mirabelle plums ripen in gold,
where sunlight dances through the leaves,
down the dirt road where your laughter once echoed.

Let's go back, hand in hand,
where time slows, and the trees remember us.
We will chase the wind like we used to,
eyes scanning the forest floor—
for mushrooms shaped like tiny umbrellas,
for four-leaf clovers whispering luck,
for wiggling worms and rabbits tucked in brambles.

Let's do it all again—
but this time, I will hold you close,
shield you like the towering oaks,
promise you more wild, carefree moments,
where your heart can heal,
and your spirit can roam free.

I will keep searching for beauty
in the cracks of my pain—
like wildflowers pushing through stone,
like light spilling through the trees at dusk.

I will mend what was never mine to break,
sew the torn edges with golden thread,
turn the wreckage into something worth keeping.

I will keep walking,
step by step, through rain and thorns,
because I was never meant to drown
in the storm someone else created.

Watch me—
turn this sorrow into soil,
let new roots take hold,
and bloom something breathtaking,
for myself.

Spring is finally stirring—
I feel it in the hush of the breeze,
in the way the earth exhales after a long winter's rest.

Buds unfurl like whispered promises,
soft petals push through the soil,
reaching for the golden touch of the sun.

Gentler days are ahead,
like rivers thawing, like birds returning home.
And soon—
I will see you again,
where the wildflowers bloom,
where warmth lingers in the air,
where our laughter will rise like the wind.

I can't wait.

Through the darkest storms,
you have held my hand—
a steady presence,
like the sun behind the clouds,
like roots gripping earth through the fiercest winds.

You have always guided me toward the light,
and now,
you tell me you're finally coming home.

Oh, the love swelling in my chest—
it spills like wildflowers breaking through frost,
like rivers rushing to meet the sea.

There is so much I long to tell you—
how I have held on,
how I have grown,
how even in the ache, I have bloomed.

Only a few more days,
and we are there.

*this poem was inspired by BTS coming home in June 2025.*

I dream of a garden in bloom,
where the air hums with the scent of jasmine,
where sunlight spills through tangled branches,
painting golden patches on the earth.

A place where I can run free,
not to escape, but to wander—
to trace the veins of a leaf,
to watch a butterfly waltz on the breeze,
to lose myself in the quiet wonder of it all.

I dream of trees heavy with fruit,
branches bending in welcome.
Bushes bursting with berries,
sweet and sun-kissed,
waiting to be gathered by gentle hands.

I dream of strawberries warm from the vine,
of bare feet sinking into the cool embrace of grass,
of dandelions scattering wishes into the wind.

Not a perfect garden,
but a living, breathing sanctuary—
wild, soft, and full of light.
A place that is truly *hygge*.

Here's to dancing barefoot in the rain,
arms wide open, heart unchained,
so full of love, it spills over—
a river too wild to be contained.

Here's to laughter echoing in golden light,
to sunshine warming your skin like a gentle promise,
to kisses soft as summer winds.

Here's to planting new seeds,
letting go of the ones that never bloomed,
making space for the flowers meant for you.

Here's to speaking your truth,
to standing tall in the story of *you*—
because you matter.
You always have.
And I hope, in some small way,
I matter to you too.

The seasons are shifting,
a quiet promise carried on the wind.
The air is softer now,
snowdrops peeking through frostbitten earth,
whispering—*spring is near.*

The trees hold their breath,
small buds pressing forward,
waiting for the sun's embrace.
I, too, am waiting—
for warmth, for light,
for the return of laughter carried on the breeze.

Life has been heavy,
its weight pressing against my ribs,
but still, I walk.
And I know you do, too.

You are not alone.
Step by step,
breath by breath,
we move toward the day
when we will be free—
free to roam,
free to love,
free to feel the shifting tides of life
without fear.

May these words find you well,
like the first blossoms of spring,
like sunlight after a long, dark winter.

*this poem was written as a response to a letter Kim Namjoon (of BTS) wrote.*

I hope you fall in love—
with the scent of wildflowers after the rain,
with chamomile's hush,
and lavender's lullaby in the evening breeze.

I hope you fall in love—
with the earth, damp and rich beneath your fingertips,
with the rhythm of raindrops
tapping secrets against your windowpane.

I hope you fall in love—
with birds tracing poetry across the sky,
with the sun spilling gold over quiet mornings,
with the moon pulling tides,
guiding you home in the dark.

I hope you fall in love
with the smallest things,
with the way life hums all around you—
soft, steady, waiting to be noticed.

I hope you fall in love
with being alive.

Oh, lavender,
bathe me in your calming scent,
let your violet blooms whisper peace
into the creases of my weary mind.

Steady my breath,
soften my sorrow,
wrap me in the warmth of your gentle embrace.

With every breeze,
let my worries drift like petals,
as you mend the wounds of my past,
one fragrant breath at a time.

From the murky depths, you rise,
petals untouched, pure as dawn.
The mud does not define you—
it only feeds your strength.

At sunrise, open wide,
let love pour in like golden light,
bloom without fear,
and when night falls,
rest in knowing—
you will be reborn again tomorrow.

I am broken still,
a stem with its bud severed,
reaching for the sun despite the wound.

But I am not broken down.
Even cut branches sprout anew,
even fallen petals nourish the earth.
This is how we grow.

If I wound you with the thorns I've carried,
forgive me—
I am learning softness again.

Hold me gently,
don't let me go.

*this poem was inspired by the song 'The Pilot </3' from ONE OK ROCK.*

When I ran,
I wasn't just fleeing from you,
from the pain,
I was searching for home—
wherever home may be.

I've grown used to solitude,
a lone wildflower swaying in the wind,
rooted in quiet, untouched fields.
But when I close my eyes,
I still reach for what was never mine—
your love,
your warm embrace,
the safety I once dreamed of.

You took that from me.
But time, like the rain, has softened the earth,
and within myself,
I have planted a sanctuary.
I have found my safe and sound.
I have found my home.
Myself.

More often than not,
I've feared the shifting winds,
the tremble of new beginnings,
the unknown path stretching beyond my feet.

I've clung to the familiar,
like roots gripping tightly to the earth,
afraid to break free,
afraid to reach for the sky.

But I've always known—
*that's where the magic happens.*
At the very edge of fear,
where the caterpillar dares the cocoon,
where the river meets the sea,
where the seed pushes through the dark,
unraveling into bloom.

And when I finally take that step,
I see the truth:
*I am stronger than I knew.*
Because wouldn't staying the same
be even scarier than the unknown?

Did you know—
if you whisper softly to the flowers,
the roses will bloom a little brighter,
the vines will reach a little higher,
the leaves will dance with the wind?

I wonder, love,
what would happen
if you spoke that gently to yourself?

If you nourished your soul
with kindness,
like rain quenching thirsty roots,
like sunlight cradling new buds—
would you not also grow?

Would you not unfurl,
petal by petal,
into something breathtaking?

I'm done being the quiet wallflower,
sitting pretty, unseen,
no more.
I won't be your delicate blossom.
Thorns, sharp and fierce,
I've outgrown that softness.

You tried to bury me,
toss me into your mess of dirt,
thinking I'd wilt,
but watch this—
I'll rise from the filth you smothered me with,
a wild thing, unshaken,
thriving in this chaos you gave me.

It's not about being 'good' anymore,
it's about strength,
about the wildflower growing through the cracks,
breaking the surface and reaching for the sun.

And oh,
it's about to get *beautifully* nasty.

*this poem was inspired by the song 'NASTY' from ONE OK ROCK.*

You can't control me anymore.
Your shadow once loomed, heavy as overgrown vines,
twisting around my roots, stealing my light.
But I am not yours to wither.

With steady hands, I prune you away,
clip by clip, I make space for new growth.
No longer weighed down, no longer stifled,
I breathe, I stretch, I rise.

Without you, the sun finds me,
the rain soaks into my soil,
and I bloom—wild, radiant,
just as I was always meant to.

I want to scream—
stand atop the highest peak,
let my voice echo through the valley,
unraveling the knots in my chest.

Let the wind take it,
tear my pain from my ribs,
scatter it like dandelion seeds,
far, far away from me.

In the space it leaves behind,
let wildflowers root,
let something new bloom—
strong, untamed, and free.

What you've been through
does not define you—
It does not make you weak.
Your journey through the fire,
through tangled thorns and shadowed woods,
has shaped you, yes—
but it has not broken you.

From the ashes, you've risen—
resilient as wildflowers
pushing through cracked earth,
courageous as roots
wrapping around stone,
strong as the oak
that bends but does not break.

I know you may not feel proud
of the scars or the weary heart
that carried you through.
But you've made it—
through storm and silence,
through nights when the world felt too heavy.

You are still here,
a living testament
to the power of perseverance.
And for that,
I'm proud of you.
Like the sun returning after the longest night,
you've shown that even in darkness,
you can find a way to bloom.

Self-care and boundaries—
roots anchoring you to the earth,
branches reaching toward the sun,
tools you should never forget.

They help you recharge,
like rainfall soaking the soil,
keeping you grounded,
and blossoming from within.

I know your heart aches
to nurture every wilting flower,
to heal every broken stem,
to make sure the garden thrives.

But remember—
you must tend to your own roots first,
water your own petals,
let sunlight warm your own leaves.

Carrying the weight of every garden
will leave your own flowers drooping,
your own soil dry and cracked.
Looking after yourself isn't selfish—
it's how you continue to bloom.

I cherish the quiet—
my mind, a garden at dawn,
where solitude blooms
and peace takes root.

Being alone with myself
is how I nurture my soul,
a place where thoughts
can stretch and unfurl
like morning glories
reaching for the sun.

Whether I'm reading,
writing stories in the shade,
listening to music
that flows like a gentle stream,
or tending to my real garden,
hands in the soil,
heart in the earth—
I find comfort in my own company.

These moments,
soft and unspoken,
are where I recharge,
where I connect with the essence
of who I am—
a wildflower growing freely,
content to bloom alone.

When life feels good,
and happiness wraps around me
like warm sunlight on a spring morning,
I find myself glancing back,
eyes searching the shadows,
waiting for the other shoe to drop—
as if joy were a fragile petal,
bound to fall.

Somewhere deep,
I hold this feeling:
that I don't quite deserve the calm,
so I plan and plan—
maps upon maps
of possible outcomes,
from A to D,
just to feel
like I'm steering the storm.

It's helped me before—
this constant guard,
this dance of hyper-vigilance,
but it's draining,
like carrying a heavy pack
while walking through wild meadows,
too burdened to notice
the flowers blooming underfoot.

Now I'm learning to loosen my grip,
to let the wind blow where it may,
trusting myself
to face whatever comes.
There is no danger,
not here, not now.
And when the storms do gather,

I know I will stand firm,
rooted and resilient.

I no longer want to live
always looking over my shoulder—
I want to live lightly,
like a leaf dancing downstream,
trusting the river to carry me
from one moment to the next.

I never thought I was resilient—
not until my therapist looked at me,
eyes steady, words soft as new leaves:
*"You're still here.*
*You've been through hell,*
*but you're still here."*

I stared at her,
a seed of doubt cracking open,
*"What else was I supposed to do?"*
And she smiled, like sunlight breaking through,
*"You and I both know*
*you could have chosen differently,*
*at any point—*
*but you chose to stay,*
*to keep growing through the cracks."*

Her words wrapped around me,
like vines finding their way to light.
*"You show up,*
*every day,*
*for yourself.*
*Even when the voices in your mind*
*whispered of giving up—*
*you kept pushing through the soil,*
*reaching for the sky."*

Something shifted inside,
like spring breaking through winter's chill—
for the first time,
I felt it.
Felt the strength deep in my bones,
rooted in every breath,
every morning I chose to rise.
Proud.

Resilient.
Like a wildflower
that refuses to be crushed.

*this poem was inspired by one of my many sessions with my therapist. These
were not her exact words, but the essence of what she told me and what I took
from it.*

Say it with me:
I am no longer available
for storms that uproot me,
for droughts that leave me empty,
for hands that only take,
but never help me grow.

I choose the sun-warmed soil,
the gentle rain,
the soft places where wildflowers bloom—
where I can breathe,
where I can be.

I am no longer available
for things that make me wither.

I didn't want to let you go.
I wanted you to turn back,
to see the garden I grew
from the ashes you left behind.

I wanted you to feel the wind shift,
to hear my laughter rise like birdsong,
to see how I've flourished
without your shadow over me.

I wanted you to regret leaving—
but now, standing in the sun,
I realize I never needed you to look back.

Because I am blooming,
and that is enough.

Be who you are—
unapologetically, fiercely so.
You are the only you this world will ever know,
why not bloom in the space you were meant to fill?

For years, they called me "quirky,"
a word that once felt like a weed in my garden,
something to be plucked, hidden,
a label that curled my petals inward.

But today, I see it differently.
We were never meant to be the same.
A field of wildflowers does not envy the oak.

So now, at thirty-something,
I stand at the edge of rediscovery,
planting new seeds where self-doubt once grew.
It's daunting—yes—
like the first green shoot breaking through the soil.
But also thrilling,
to stretch toward the light and finally fall in love with *me*.

I am on a journey—
to teach myself kindness,
to water the roots I once neglected.

For years, I punished myself,
pushed and pruned away my own needs,
trying to shape myself into something
that would make others stay.

But in pleasing them,
I forgot the sound of my own voice,
the rhythm of my own heart,
the feeling of the sun on my skin.

I withered in the shadows,
a flower too afraid to reach for the light.

No more.

It may feel selfish at first,
foreign, even—
to place my hands on my own soil
and tend to what I need.

But I will grow,
and those who truly love me
will not fear my bloom.
They will stand in the garden beside me,
grateful for the way I shine.

I hope your future
unfolds like wildflowers in spring,
soft and unhurried,
bathed in golden light.

May love find you gently,
like the whisper of morning dew,
and joy root itself deep within you,
steady as an ancient tree.

May you bloom freely,
your petals open wide,
dancing in the warmth
of the sun's embrace.

We are seekers of the sun,
turning toward its golden glow,
like wildflowers stretching skyward,
yearning for warmth.

And you—
you are the human definition of sunlight,
spilling gold into shadowed spaces,
lifting weary hearts,
warming even the coldest days.

Thank you for being you,
for shining without knowing,
for radiating light in ways
you may never see—
but are felt, deeply,
by those who stand in your glow.

You are appreciated
more than you'll ever know.

*this poem was inspired by Jung Hoseok (of BTS).*

It rained for days,
the sky weeping in quiet sorrow.
It rained for months,
puddles reflecting the weight of the storm.
It rained for years,
roots drowning, the earth heavy with grief.

But now—
look at the fields bursting with color,
petals kissed by the past,
rivers running softer,
the world washed clean.

Look at all the pretty flowers.

You might feel guilt,
like a storm cloud pressing heavy on your chest.
But remember why
you built this boundary—
why you planted this line in the earth.

Let the guilt settle,
seep into the soil like rain,
nourishing the roots of your strength.
Then rise—
with the fire of self-worth in your veins,
with the sun on your back,
unshaken, unwavering.

You can do this.
Keep your boundary.

You are making me so proud.
Not because you are strong,
but because you are gentle—
with yourself, with the world,
with the feelings you once feared.

You no longer run from them.
You welcome them like rain,
knowing they will pass,
knowing they will nourish you in time.

Like the trees trust the wind,
like the flowers lean toward the sun,
you've learned to sit with yourself,
to breathe, to listen, to let go.

Isn't that amazing?
Damn, you're amazing.
Yeah, you!

This is your season to bloom,
and I swear,
your soul has never looked more radiant.

We are seekers of the moon,
drawn to its quiet glow,
finding solace in silver light
when the world turns dark.

In the night, we do not shrink—
we *roar*, we *bloom*,
our roots deepening in the soil of our souls,
our branches reaching for the stars.

We do not run from our feelings;
we sit with them beneath the vast sky,
listening to the whispers of the wind,
knowing that even in darkness,
*we matter, we grow, we shine.*

*this poem was inspired by Park Jimin (of BTS).*

I want to dance in the rain,
let the droplets kiss my skin,
each one a whispered secret from the sky,
I want to feel the cool, sweet air fill my lungs,
as I spin—
wild and untamed.

The rain splashes around me,
a symphony of nature's joy,
pattering on the earth,
a reminder that life can be messy,
but oh, how it grows.

In this moment,
I am free—
untethered by the weight of worry,
my soul a leaf carried by the breeze,
light as the rain,
and as alive as the earth beneath my feet.

You are stronger than you realize,
even when the storms rage inside.
I know you don't believe it now,
but in time, you'll see the truth—
the quiet resilience you carry,
like the roots that hold the tallest trees,
even in the fiercest winds.

Look at how far you've come,
each step a victory,
every scar a testament to your strength,
a mark of survival.
You've weathered so much and still,
you rise with the sun each day,
even when the night seems endless.

Don't reopen those old wounds.
Protect your peace,
like the way the forest protects its delicate blooms,
nurturing what's new, what's tender,
while guarding against the harshness of the world.
You've done your best,
and you will continue to grow,
just as the earth heals,
one season at a time.

Like a thorny rosebush,
I have to cut you away—
not out of cruelty,
but so I do not bleed myself dry.

Some things must be pruned
for the petals to bloom,
for the roots to breathe,
for life to continue.

And though it stings,
I know—
what is meant to grow, will grow.

Sometimes,
I wonder, *why am I like this?*
I curse the weight I carry,
the storm that lives beneath my skin.

But then I remember—
this was never my fault.
Trauma left its fingerprints,
etched itself into my bones.
Yes, I was a sensitive child,
but pain wove the vines of anxiety,
the shadowed roots of depression.

Still—
even in the mud, the lotus rises.
I am no different.
Every day, I reach,
petals unfolding, inching toward the sun,
working with what I have,
not just to survive—
but to bloom.

Because I am more than what broke me.

*this poem was inspired by Min Yoongi (of BTS).*

As a child,
every choice felt like a tightrope—
one wrong step, and I'd fall into silence,
locked behind my own ribs.
Yes or no?
Speak my truth and face his fury,
or shrink myself, small and safe,
so the storm would pass over me?

Even now, my voice wavers like a brittle leaf,
torn between the wind and the weight of others.
I've spent years shaping myself
to fit their comfort—
so my father wouldn't rage,
so my mother wouldn't grieve,
so my sister wouldn't suffer.

But seasons change,
and so do I.
No longer a rootless thing,
I plant myself firm in the soil of my own truth.
I will listen when my body whispers,
*"This will drain you."*
I will honor the weight in my chest that says,
*"Not this time."*

It is not selfish to bloom,
to let my own petals unfurl first,
before tending to the gardens of others.
I am not selfish—
I am simply learning
to love myself.

*"It's all my fault,"*
a sentence I've whispered to myself
so many times, it became my shadow,
woven into my every breath.
For years, I carried it—
a stone pressed into my chest.
And sometimes, I still do.

But I'm learning.
It was never mine to hold.
I was not a failure
for the way their happiness slipped through my fingers,
like sand too restless to stay.
I was not a failure
for being a daughter who bloomed differently,
for not fitting the mold,
for dreaming too big,
even when they said, *"you can be anything."*

I have spent my life apologizing
for the space I take up,
for the air I breathe,
for the way my voice wavers
or my hands hesitate.
*Sorry for speaking.*
*Sorry for standing here.*
*Sorry for simply existing.*

But the earth does not apologize
when spring spills over its edges,
when wildflowers take root in forgotten places.
And neither will I.

I see it now—
I was never meant to be small.

I have never been good
at asking for help—
I'd rather be the steady tree,
rooted, offering shade to others.

I love helping—
watering the dry gardens
of those I love,
but when it comes to me,
I hold back—
afraid that asking
might mean I'll lose something,
that giving in
means a part of me
will wither away.

Because that's what I learned as a child—
help was conditional,
like a drought that followed every rain,
and it was always
a one-way street.

It's still hard—
opening up, letting people
water the roots I've kept hidden.
But I'm learning
that not everyone
is a storm to fear—
some are soft rains,
nourishing the soil
of my heart.

There's no shame
in asking for help—
it doesn't mean I'm weak.

It means that some burdens
are too heavy
for one pair of hands
to carry alone.

And that's okay.
I am learning
to ask for rain—
to let the world
pour kindness into my roots,
so I, too, can bloom.

For a long time,
I've learned to listen to the quiet whispers of life.
The way sunlight dances through the trees,
a golden ribbon weaving through emerald leaves.
The rhythm of raindrops tapping on my window,
a lullaby from the sky, soft and steady.
The wind, carrying secrets from distant places,
whistling through the branches,
and the tiny creatures of the forest—
unseen, but always present,
their lives unfolding in the shadows of towering trees.

I watch the earth,
where tender roots push through the soil,
where plants stretch toward the sky,
a quiet, unspoken miracle.

In these small, sacred moments,
I find solace.
The act of slowing, of breathing,
fills me with light and energy,
as if the world itself is healing me
with each breath I take.

Even when life feels heavy,
the earth reminds me—
there is always beauty,
always peace,
waiting for me in the quiet corners of the world.
It's here, in the smallest things,
that I find my strength to keep going.

It's okay to ask for support,
like the young apple tree,
rooted but fragile,
its slender stem sways
in the unforgiving wind.

It doesn't shrink in shame
when you place a sturdy stake
beside it—
a quiet companion
holding its dreams upright.
Seasons sweep through,
cold rains, wild storms,
and the tree leans, learns,
wrapped in the gentle embrace
of support that never scolds.

And slowly, with each dawn,
the tree grows stronger,
its roots deepening,
leaves whispering secrets
of resilience and light.

One day, the stake is gone,
left behind in soft soil,
and in its place—
a canopy of blossoms,
petals kissing the air,
soft perfume of becoming
carried on the breeze.

It's okay to need a hand—
even nature knows
that growth is not always
a solitary bloom.

I am my truest self
when I let the world slow down,
when I pause to breathe
and savor life's smallest moments.
The flutter of a bird's wings,
the way the sunlight spills like liquid gold
over the edges of trees,
the whisper of wind through the leaves—
these are the moments I live for.

It's in the stillness I find my strength,
in the peace of quiet mornings,
wrapped in the arms of nature,
where I reconnect with my roots.
Here, in this sacred space,
I rediscover my own light—
soft, yet radiant,
filling the spaces around me,
and I can see how much I've grown.

I could never surrender these moments
to the humdrum of endless work,
to days that feel like machines,
churning on without pause.
No, I choose to embrace life,
to live with intention,
to honor the rhythms of nature—
the ebb and flow of the seasons
that teach me how to heal,
how to grow.

And I am humbled,
for none of this would be possible
without the love and support
of the one who walks beside me—

my heart, my partner,
my soulmate,
my husband.
For his love is the soil in which I root,
and with him, I am whole.
I am deeply, quietly grateful.

*this poem was written for my husband <3

I don't know what I'll do
when you show up—
unannounced,
like the sudden storm that rips through a quiet meadow,
when the silence has lingered too long,
and the words between us have withered,
fading like autumn leaves.

I don't know how I'll react—
but I fear the weight of that moment,
the way my breath might catch,
the way my heart might hesitate
between past hurts and present peace.
I don't want to think of that day,
but somewhere inside,
I know it's coming,
like the turning of the tide,
I can't control it.

But I hope, when it comes,
I'll be rooted,
like the ancient oak,
grounded in the soil of my healing.
I'll stand tall in the garden I've tended,
in your absence, I've learned to grow—
nurtured by silence, by stillness,
I've planted seeds of strength,
watered them with self-care,
and now I bloom in ways you've never seen.

When you arrive,
I'll protect my peace,
the sacred space I've cultivated,
not out of bitterness,
but from the love I've learned to give myself.

And if you try to tread upon it,
I'll offer no apology.
For my garden is mine to keep,
and in this quiet,
I have found my power.

For all the friends I've met along this winding path,
thank you.
Thank you for the kindness that grew between us,
like flowers blooming in the quiet corners of my heart.
For showing me love when the world seemed so cold,
for lifting me in my darkest days,
when hope felt like a distant shore.

Though miles stretch between us,
your warmth reached me like sunlight through the trees,
a steady glow that held me when I was ready to give up,
a hand extended, though you didn't know me at all.

You reminded me that each season has its beauty,
that even in the hardest winters,
there is strength to be found,
and with each other, we shine—
brighter than stars scattered across a midnight sky,
warmer than the sun after a long, cold night.

Thank you for being you—
for your kindness, your sweetness,
for the love you've shared so freely.
You may never know how much your light
has helped me through the storms,
how your presence has healed my spirit
like rain nurturing a garden.

Through the years, I've found a home here,
among you, in this community of grace.
You are the leaves in my branches,
the roots that keep me grounded.
I carry your love like the earth carries the rain—
ever nourishing, ever abundant.
I wish you the moon and stars,

the gentleness of the breeze,
and all the joy that blooms in spring,
because you deserve it all.
Thank you.

*this poem was written for all the friends I've made in the BTS community.

I'm too good at overanalyzing,
reading between the lines,
tracing patterns in the silence
like branches splitting in a winter sky.
I build stories in my head—
tangles of doubt,
roots of worry,
convincing myself I'm unloved
when friends don't respond.

But I'm learning—
learning to see the space between words
as just that—space,
not a judgment, not a dismissal,
but a quiet, like a forest
resting after a storm.
Sometimes, people retreat,
just like flowers close at dusk,
not to shut out the world,
but to gather strength in stillness.

And just as I'm learning
not to respond right away—
to take my time like a river
finding its path through stone—
I'm learning that others have their reasons too,
reasons rooted in their own soil.
It's not always about me,
and even if it is,
I can breathe through it—
in and out, like waves on a calm shore.

I'm learning to let go—
to be comfortable in the uncomfortable,
to trust the ebb and flow,

and to welcome the quiet spaces
between connection,
knowing that love,
like wildflowers in spring,
returns in its own time.

I don't have many friends—
mostly because I'm afraid
of being uprooted,
of not being seen
for the wildflower I am.

So I plant myself in solitude,
wrap my heart in layers of bark,
pretending it doesn't ache
to stretch toward the sun.
I hide among shadows,
convincing myself it's safer
to stay rooted in silence
than risk being uprooted
by rejection.

Sometimes, I hurt myself first,
before anyone else can—
like trimming my own leaves
to stop them from being torn.
But I know now—
this isn't how I'm meant to grow.

I'm learning that guarding my heart
too fiercely
keeps it from breathing,
from feeling the rain,
from soaking up kindness
like sunlight through leaves.

I want to bloom without fear,
to trust that not every touch
will break me,
that not every friend
will leave me wilted.

It's time to let go of the thorns
and allow myself
to grow toward love.

Kids are like primed seedling soil—
tender ground, where words uncoil.
what you plant will take root and grow,
in their hearts, where love will flow.

So fill them with kindness, fill them with light,
like sunlight pouring through the night.
Water them with care and grace,
and watch the bloom take its place.

In time, you'll see the beauty rise—
a garden of truth beneath their skies.
They'll treat you with the love you gave,
and in their embrace, you'll find what's saved.

One day, those tiny fingers, small and strong,
will wrap around you and sing their song:
"*You did good,*" they'll softly say,
and your heart will bloom in a bright display.

Your eyes may fill with joyful tears,
for you've nurtured them through the years.
Because you did that—you made it right,
you sowed love, and brought them light.

You paid it forward, in every way,
and watched the seeds of kindness stay.

*this poem was inspired by my kids and written for them in mind.*

Once, I was okay with fading away,
like the last leaf falling in autumn's grasp,
whispering goodbyes to the breeze.
But now, I fight for each breath,
like a seed breaking through the soil,
pushing through darkness to reach the light.

I treasure every inhale,
the way air fills my lungs,
the way each breath feels like the first raindrop
on a thirsty earth.
Because life is a gift,
a wildflower blooming in the cracks of stone,
a chance I won't let slip away.

I hold on to every moment,
like a river holds the sky's reflection—
unwavering, full of life.
I won't miss a single heartbeat,
not when the wind sings in my hair,
not when the sun kisses my skin,
not when the world is still turning
and I am here to witness it all.

If their version of family
costs you your peace,
like tangled vines choking the wildflowers,
it's not family. It's control—
a garden overrun,
where your blossoms are stifled,
your roots suffocated.

Choosing yourself isn't betrayal,
it's survival—
like a tree shedding dead branches
to thrive in the sunlight,
or a river breaking free from a dam
to flow where it's meant to go.

It's okay to let them go—
to let your garden breathe,
to reclaim your roots,
and allow peace to grow wild,
untamed and true.

Look how far you've come—
like a wildflower pushing through concrete,
you broke cycles you weren't taught to break,
untangling roots from the past,
planting seeds of change in barren soil.

You're learning to love
in ways you were never shown—
softly, like rain soaking dry earth,
gently, like sunlight kissing new leaves.
You're becoming the person
you once needed—
the shelter, the bloom, the soil and sun.

That's not just healing—
that's growth,
that's fucking courage—
breaking free from the weight of your roots
and daring to grow tall
in your own light.

Don't chase perfection—
it's a mirage in the desert,
a flower that never blooms,
and you'll only burn yourself out,
left tangled in weeds,
choking on your own expectations.

Focus on just existing—
like wildflowers that grow
without permission,
or rivers that flow
without force.
You are already enough.

You've pushed and pushed
your whole life—
try just being,
rooted in the soil of your presence,
and let life come to you—
softly, naturally,
like sunlight through the leaves.

Thank you for being here—
for standing like a steadfast tree
through every storm and season.

I love your smile—
bright as wild daisies,
reaching for the sun.

I love your energy—
a river flowing,
gentle and fierce,
always moving forward.

I love your soul—
a garden of wild beauty,
roots deep and strong,
blooming in kindness.

I love you—
in every petal,
in every sunrise,
in every breath.

Thank you—
for being you.
For being here.
For growing.

Learning to be kind to myself
was like dawn breaking through
after years of storms,
a soft light touching the bruised earth
of my soul.

For so long,
I was my own worst critic,
cutting myself down
before anyone else could—
like trimming petals
to protect the bloom,
only to find
the garden empty,
silent, and aching.

But now I know—
it is vital to nurture
the roots within,
to water the wildflowers
growing in my heart,
to offer myself
the same gentle words
I gift to others.

Self-kindness is a garden
that heals itself—
slowly, tenderly,
blossoming into something
soft,
strong,
and beautiful.

I hear you—
your voice like a trembling leaf
in the wind,
your quiet cries
echoing through the dark,
but no more
should you weep alone
in the shadowed corners
of your room.

Come here—
let me wrap you
in a hug
as warm as sunlight
on a winter morning.
We'll weather this storm together,
rooted like ancient trees
against the howling winds.

You are stronger
than you know—
a wildflower
pushing through cracks,
resilient,
blooming despite the weight
of heavy rain.

It's going to be okay—
I promise.
I'll hold you close,
little one,
and I'll never let go.
We'll find the light
together.

Slowing down—
I used to see it
as weakness,
like the bending of a flower
in the wind.
I've always chased achievement,
pushing myself to bloom
before the season was right,
convinced
I wasn't doing enough,
wasn't enough…

I am sorry.
You didn't deserve that—
the restless nights,
the constant striving,
the fear
that slowing down
would make me less.

Now,
I am learning
to move gently,
like a river
finding its way
through quiet meadows.
Relaxing
feels strange,
like the first warm breeze
after a long, harsh winter,
but I know
it's not wrong—
it's just new.

With time,

the guilt will fade
like shadows retreating
at dawn,
and my heart
will soften,
relationships
will blossom—
because taking it slow,
letting myself breathe,
is bringing me
so much joy.

I admire you—
the way you dressed
like wildflowers blooming
bold and unafraid,
the way you wrote
your heart onto paper,
raw and unguarded,
strong as roots
in the shifting earth.

Somewhere
between adolescence and adulthood,
I lost my way,
like a wandering river
dammed by doubt,
flowing too carefully,
afraid to overflow.
But I'm finding my path again,
tracing the lines
back to the core of me—
the untamed spirit,
the one who never
apologized for blooming.

I won't shrink myself
to fit into shadows
or quieter spaces—
I'll stretch toward the sun,
reclaiming the wild,
authentic me.

I admire you
for being so true
to who you were—
and I'm coming back

to that person,
to the one
who wears color
without shame,
who speaks her mind
and loves fiercely.

I will not apologize
for who I am
or what I love—
I am a wildflower
finding her way
back to the sun.

It's okay to feel anger—
even when it roars
like a storm through the trees,
even when it crashes
like waves against the shore.

You can yell,
let it echo like thunder,
let it spill like rain.
Your feelings are fierce and real—
they deserve to be heard.

Even when your winds howl,
even when your river rages,
I will be here—
a mountain unmoved,
a forest still rooted.

I won't stop loving you,
won't close my heart
or withhold my warmth.
No storm can tear apart
this safe place we've built.

Let your anger flow—
it doesn't scare me,
it doesn't change
the soil we've nurtured,
or the sun that follows.

You're allowed to feel it all,
without losing love,
without losing me.
I'll hold space for you
until the calm returns.

It's okay to make mistakes,
to stumble like the leaves in autumn,
twirling and falling with grace,
only to rise again in spring.

You are lovable in your cracks,
in your flaws,
like the weathered stones on a riverbank,
shaped by time,
but still whole,
still beautiful.

You don't have to be perfect—
like the wildflower that grows
without knowing where it will bloom,
you don't need to be flawless
for me to love you.

I love you in the moments of silence,
when you are broken and whole,
and I love you in the messy,
in the soft,
in the imperfect,
like the earth beneath our feet—
always healing,
always growing.

You don't have to do it "right,"
like a river that winds and bends,
carving its path through the earth,
not concerned with how it flows—
it simply is,
and I will love you like that.

I will love you in your quiet,
in the spaces between your words,
like the stillness of a forest,
where nothing needs to be said
for the trees to stand tall,
for the wind to whisper its song.

No matter what you say or do,
even if you say nothing at all,
my love will be as constant
as the sun rising over the mountains,
unfaltering,
warm,
ever-present.

You don't have to be perfect,
just as a flower doesn't need to bloom on command—
it blooms when it's ready,
in its own time,
and I will wait for you,
with open arms,
and a heart full of love.

You are so fucking kind,
like the gentle breeze that stirs the leaves,
like the sunlight that warms the earth—
your love flows freely,
rooted deep in the soil of your soul.

Thank you for being you,
for the quiet strength you offer,
like a river that carves its way,
unhurried, yet unstoppable.
Your heart, a garden of light,
and I am blessed to walk beside you.

In your presence, I am home,
my true self blooms,
like a wildflower kissed by the rain—
in your love, I find my roots,
strong and steady,
and I carry your kindness
with me, like sunlight in my chest.

You've never quite fit,
and for a while, that didn't trouble you.
But as the seasons changed,
you found yourself shrinking,
like a flower hiding from the sun,
trying to fit into a pot too small for your roots.

But listen—
it's not about fitting in.
It's about standing out,
like a tree in a wild forest,
not afraid to stretch its branches to the sky.
What if, by being your truest self,
you become exactly where you belong?
You'll find the soil that nurtures your growth,
the sunlight that warms your soul.

You'll belong, not by shrinking,
but by blooming,
in your own time,
in your own space.

So step back,
into the earth that calls you,
and let yourself rise,
authentically—
just like nature intended.

Nothing in nature blooms all year—
even the wildflowers rest.
So why should you expect yourself
to be in full bloom, always?

Life moves in cycles:
the sun rises,
the moon wanes,
the trees shed to grow again.

Even the storm has purpose.
Even stillness is sacred.
So be gentle with yourself
when all you manage is a breath,
a single step,
a moment of pause.

Tiny steps, like soft rain,
will nourish your roots.
And one day,
without even noticing,
you'll find yourself
blooming again.

It's okay—not to be okay.
Even the sun hides behind clouds.
Even the earth slows in winter's hush.

Some days will feel heavy.
Your body may ask for stillness,
your mind may crave silence.
That's not weakness—
it's wisdom.

So breathe.
Slow down, like the tide retreating.
Curl inward like a fern at dusk.
Rest is not retreat,
it's regeneration.

Wrap your arms around yourself
like the wind cradles the leaves.
This pause—
this quiet—
is not wasted time.

It's how you grow again.
So please, don't neglect yourself.
The world needs the you
who blooms from care.

Be soft—
if not for yourself,
then just to defy the storm he tried to build in you.
He wanted you to sharpen your edges,
to armor your heart with thorns,
and hide your softness behind walls.
But softness is not a flaw—
it's a strength,
a quiet power that blooms in the quiet spaces,
like flowers that grow through cracks in the concrete.

Having feelings isn't weakness,
it's the root of your humanity.
It's the stream that nurtures your spirit,
the wind that whispers to your soul.
He wanted you to be like him,
but you are nothing like him.
You are you,
a force of nature,
and I love you for that.

Be proud of your feelings,
of the way your heart sways with the seasons.
Honor your intuition,
like a tree that listens to the wind,
and bends without breaking.
Follow your gut—
it has never steered you wrong,
it is the ancient wisdom of the earth,
whispering that you are enough.
Trust yourself.
For you, like nature, will always find your way back
to the light.

Autumn tiptoes in, painting the garden with shades of
amber and rust. Sunshine feels the crispness in the air,
a whispered reminder that change is near. She's ready,
though—prepared with seedlings for the winter, a promise
of life that will stretch through the colder months.
Yet, her heart still clings to the summer blooms that linger,
holding on just a little longer.

With gentle hands, Sunshine moves among the
fading flowers, murmuring gratitude for their colors and
the joy they've brought. It's almost time to say goodbye,
to gather their seeds and let them rest. Carefully, she cradles
each bloom, coaxing the seeds free and storing them in tiny
brown paper bags. Each bag bears a hand-drawn doodle,
a quirky little sketch of the plant it holds, like a love letter
to the summer past. Some seeds need to dry first, so she lays
them out on a windowsill, where the last golden rays of sun
can kiss them dry.
As winter creeps closer, she knows it's time to let the old
plants go. One by one, she pulls them up, whispering
thanks as their roots release from the soil. Into the compost
bin they go—a resting place where they will break down
and become rich, fertile soil. It's a bittersweet ritual, but
Sunshine knows it's necessary. The garden, like life itself,
is a cycle—birth, bloom, rest, and renewal.

She takes a moment to breathe in the earthy scent,
the way the leaves crunch softly underfoot, and feels a calm
settle in her chest. It's not just the end—it's a new
beginning wrapped in soil and seed, decay and hope.

These old plants will feed the next generation, helping new flowers and vegetables reach for the sun come spring.

As she gathers the last of the seeds, Sunshine smiles, feeling rooted in the rhythm of the earth. Her garden rests, but it's not truly asleep—it's simply dreaming of what comes next.

I find joy in the little things—
the golden light filtering through the trees,
the laughter of our children echoing like birdsong,
the quiet kindness in the way you move through this world.

You have shown me that love can be soft,
that trust does not always come with a price.
I was taught that love was fragile, fleeting,
a thing to be earned, to be bargained for.
But you—
you love without conditions, without cages.

You leave me notes when my own voice falters,
whispers written on paper—
You are worthy.
You are loved.
Like sunlight breaking through the canopy,
your love reaches the places I once thought untouchable.

And when we falter, when we fall,
we do not shatter—
we mend, we learn, we grow like roots intertwining,
stronger than before.

You are the best thing that has ever happened to me,
not a fleeting moment, not a passing storm,
but a constant, like the tide, like the turning of the earth.

Thank you—
for your hands, your heart, your unwavering light.
*Thank you, for you.*


*this poem was written for my husband <3*

a garden
in bloom

Thank you, from the depths of my heart, for reading my
poems. You have no idea how much it means to me—truly.
I hope, in some small way, these words found their way to
you like sunlight filtering through leaves, like a gentle breeze
carrying a whisper of comfort. I hope something here
resonated with you, stirred something inside you, made
you feel seen, understood, held. I hope, even if just for a
moment, you felt less alone in the vastness of your thoughts
and emotions.

Since childhood, writing has been my refuge, my compass.
My teachers once thought I would grow up to be a writer,
and maybe—just maybe—I will. I don't know where this
path will lead, but I do know this: I needed these poems.
I need something tangible to hold onto when doubt creeps
in, when the weight of the world feels too heavy. This book
is my reminder, my lighthouse in the dark, something I can
reach for when I need to feel warmth and reassurance.
If, by some miracle, it can offer the same to you—to even
one person—then I will be the happiest soul alive.

I have always dreamed of writing a book.
And though this may not be the book that eight-year-old
me envisioned, it is the book she needs. Perhaps, one day,
all the fantastical stories I dreamed up will take flight, but
for now, this—this raw, open-hearted collection of words—
is what my soul needed to bring into the world.

Poetry has always been my way of journaling, of turning
fleeting emotions into something real. Some of these poems
began as songs, others started as whispers in the margins of
my notebooks, and some I have reshaped, given them new
wings, a more hopeful voice than the ones they carried in
my teenage years when life felt unbearably heavy.

My inspiration comes from nature, from the slow and
steady rhythm of gardening, from the music that has
wrapped around me like a second skin. These things,

along with the unwavering love of my family, have shaped
me, kept me breathing, kept me whole.
And I want to take a moment to share my deepest gratitude
with the artists who unknowingly carried me through my
darkest days. To BTS—Kim Namjoon, Kim Seokjin,
Min Yoongi, Jung Hoseok, Park Jimin, Kim Taehyung,
and Jeon Jungkook—thank you. When the world felt too
sharp, your words were a soft place to land. You reminded
me that *"it's gonna be alright,"* that even when I fall,
I can rise again, and that no matter how lost I feel,
I am never truly alone.

To ONE OK ROCK—Takahiro Moriuchi,
Toru Yamashita, Tomoya Kanki, and Ryota Kohama—
you've been the soundtrack to my survival.
Taka, the words you write—I don't even know where to
begin. But knowing that someone across the world has felt
what I have felt, has woven pain into something beautiful—
it gave me comfort when I needed it most. Their songs have
broken me open and healed me in equal measure.

And then there is AURORA—her ethereal voice, her raw
authenticity, the poetry of her music. She reminds me to
embrace myself fully, wildly, unapologetically without fear
or shame.

I know that what speaks to my soul might not resonate
with yours, but if you ever need something to hold onto,
if you are searching for something to stir your heart,
I urge you to give these artists a chance. Music does not
need a shared spoken language to be understood;
it transcends borders, wraps around you like a whispered
truth. And if you do take the time to look up the
translations, you might just find words that feel like home.
And lastly, to the ones who have always been there—

To my family, to my friends, those who have stood by me through every season of my life. I want to thank you from the very core of my being, for your love, your patience, your unwavering support. You are the roots that have kept me grounded, the sunshine that has warmed my soul on the coldest days. My husband, my children—*you are my heart, my home, my world.* My life is infinitely richer with you by my side, like a garden made vibrant by your presence. You have made every moment worth living.

And to all the friends I have been fortunate enough to meet along this journey—whether in the tangible world or the digital one—we are all connected by invisible threads, woven together by shared experiences, laughter, and understanding. Please know, from the deepest part of me, that I treasure you. *You matter more to me than words could ever fully express.* Your kindness, your authenticity, and your light have been guiding stars on my path, and I will carry that with me always.

Thank you. For being you. For sharing your love, your strength, your warmth. You have made my life not just bearable, but beautiful.

I'm not the best at goodbyes, but I suppose this is where I must end. So once more, from the deepest roots of my being, thank you. Thank you for holding these pages in your hands, for giving my words a place to land. I hope, in some way, this book can be a light on your healing journey—or a gift for someone who may need it more than you know.

And above all else, please remember this:

**you are loved, you matter, and you are a beautiful garden in bloom.**

**A final whisper, from one sprout to another**

If you—or someone you care about—are wandering through the fog of depression, anxiety, self-harm, or thoughts that feel too heavy to carry alone, please, reach out. Whether it's a hand you know well—a friend, a family member—or a kind soul online who reminds you that light still exists... or maybe, most importantly, a professional who's trained to help you find the path back to yourself.

Storms don't last forever. Not even the fiercest ones.

Whatever you're facing, however tangled or wild it may seem, you are *not* alone. Your feelings are real, but they are not all there is. There is still softness in the world. Still sun after rain. Still soil where something beautiful can grow.

You are worthy of healing.

Of joy.

Of mornings that don't ache.

And somewhere, a new beginning is already stretching toward the light—just for you.